*How to Survive
the Age of Travel*

Also by Robert Thomas Allen

WE GAVE YOU THE ELECTRIC TOOTHBRUSH
CHILDREN, WIVES, AND OTHER WILDLIFE

How to Survive the Age of Travel

155391

Robert Thomas Allen

Doubleday and Canada Limited, Toronto, Ontario
Doubleday & Company, Inc., Garden City, New York
1974

Grateful acknowledgment is made to the following for permission to excerpt from the articles included in this book:

The Canadian Magazine: "Village," September 10, 1970, "Trappists," January 17, 1970, "General Store," September 12, 1970. Copyright © 1970 by The Canadian Magazine.

Canadian Homes: "Florida," November 1966. Copyright © 1966 by Canadian Homes.

Canadian Weekly: "La Salle," March 27, 1965. Copyright © 1965 by Canadian Weekly.

Imperial Review: "Motor Trip," originally entitled, "But I Like Motor Trips," Issue 3, 1972.

Maclean's Magazine: "Hardy" and "Bath," March 20, 1965, "Fiji," February 1971, "Greece," May 1969, "Charters," February 1973, "Announcements." Copyright © 1965, 1969, 1971, 1973 by Maclean's Magazine.

Panorama: "Barns," June 17, 1972, "Homesickness," June 19, 1972, "Book Sale," July 1, 1972, "Champlain," July 22, 1972, "Parliament," August 5, 1972, "Zoo," August 12, 1972, "Language," August 19, 1972, "Hardware," September 9, 1972, "Einstein," November 4, 1972, "Car Sickness," November 18, 1972, "Hotels," December 30, 1972, "Conventions," January 27, 1973, "Florida," February 17, 1973, "Seagulls," March 24, 1973, "Church," March 31, 1973, "Drugstore," April 7, 1973, "Jerusalem," April 21, 1973, "Citzenship," May 5, 1973, "Bagpipes," May 10, 1973, "Rocket," June 2, 1973, "Airport," June 23, 1973, "Glaciers," July 7, 1973. Copyright © 1972, 1973 by The Canadian Star Weekly. Reprinted by permission of *The Canadian Star Weekly.*

The Sunday Sun: "Orient," from articles originally entitled, "Being at the Real Source of Things," March 3, 1974, "The Men Destroyed the Mellow Mood," March 10, 1974, "Streetcar Meditations on Buddha and Bible," March 17, 1974, "Chemin de fer, Craps and Keno," March 24, 1974 and "Greeting 'old friends' in Japanese Guise," April 14, 1974.

Toronto Life Magazine: "Cherry Beach," originally entitled, "On The Beach," June 1974. Copyright © 1974 by Toronto Life Magazine.

The Toronto Star: "Old City," August 19, 1964, "Zoo," October 7, 1964, "Ripley, Eng," January 19, 1965, "Sitting," January 28, 1965, "Pubs," February 8, 1965, "Cold Rooms," February 11, 1965, "Tipping," February 18, 1965, "Niagara," originally entitled, "My Favorite Cruise, only $1.15," May 20, 1965. Copyright © 1964, 1965 by The Toronto Star.

Library of Congress Cataloging in Publication Data
Allen, Robert Thomas.
   How to survive the age of travel.
    1. Voyages and travels—1951–   —Anecdotes, facetiae, satire, etc.   I. Title.
G464.A42 1975   910'.202
ISBN 0-385-09684-4
Library of Congress Catalog Card Number 74-2713

To *MARY, JANE*
AND *FLOYD*

Contents

x   *Contents*

*How to Survive
the Age of Travel*

1

Get Your Teeth Fixed
in View of the Parthenon

Now that the energy shortage has made us all pay attention to things we haven't thought of for years, like where electricity and gasoline come from, there's a good chance we'll take a closer look at world travel—and our freedom to take off for anywhere, any time, as long as we have the money. Unexpected changes have already taken place in motor travel. Most people driving in regions where highway speeds have been lowered to fifty-five miles an hour, are delighted with it, including me.

My generation started driving in an era when motorists gripped the wheel with white knuckles at speeds over forty miles an hour. By imperceptible degrees we changed with the times until we were cruising at eighty miles an hour, with local housewives, off to nearby shopping plazas, passing us at ninety with their hair in curlers. Yet right after the world started running short of gas, my wife and I drove from Toronto to Florida at fifty-five miles an hour. It seemed to take no longer than when we drove it at eighty. We felt as if we were going very fast, in fact; and we steered with the same great skill, making smooth turns, taking pride in balancing a thermos top of coffee on the instrument panel. Everyone I talked to on the road felt the same, with the exception of one man from New York to whom I got talking in a motel in Marietta, Georgia. He told me that after driving over 800 miles at fifty-five miles an hour, he'd had a sudden urge for speed, and rammed his car up to 100 miles an hour on a long straight stretch in Georgia, just in time to pass a cop who was hiding behind a grove of Georgia pine waiting for something interesting to happen.

But most tourists adjusted easily, and perhaps the same thing will happen in relation to all kinds of travel. Not that a Boeing 747, say, will slow down from 550 miles an hour to fifty-five, for if it did it would fall, but the inner clockwork of the passengers will slow down. If we have to take fewer trips, we'll start to take a better look at the world, instead of trying to lasso it in Kodachrome (I remember one woman in Holland looking at a picturesque herd of Holsteins; she turned to her husband, who was fumbling for a new film, dropping things, and said coldly: "Why don't you just LOOK at them—JUST ONCE!"). Then the kind of travel promoter who has been getting more and more desperate for new travel gimmicks, and getting closer to ideas like Dental Tours—"Get your teeth fixed in view of the Parthenon"—may disappear. I hope that something that will disappear along with him will be the conviction, held by most of us, that things will always go along pretty much as they always have.

If that happens we won't hear as often as we do now the expression "You can't stop progress," a neat little proposition with a couple of loose premises, if not a blown head gasket—and which has as a corollary the idea that anyone who tries to stop anything is mired in the past. This change will be a triumph both for young liberals and cranky old men who are frequently told, "If everyone thought the way you do, we'd still be using bows and arrows," which conjures up images of hide-bound old cave men muttering, "Nothing will ever replace the good old rock." TV-commercial writers, who manage to get hold of the wrong end of things oftener than the members of any other profession, often use hints of senile perversity to prove, for example, that instant coffee is just like real coffee, when everybody knows it tastes like boiled bark. Refusing to drink it is not a sign of age, but of unimpaired taste buds, and a heroic spirit of independence. Now that instant travel may have to be taken off the shelves, we all may come to realize that journeys don't get better the faster and oftener you take them—and we may go back to the days when travel was a special treat, took time, even cost more, but was something to savor at leisure. We may even discover that a place does not necessarily become more interesting the farther away it is from the place we're in.

The Romance of Perfume,
Wet Willow Leaves and Anthracite

When Tom Pocock, the travel editor of the London *Evening Standard*, pleaded with the travel industry to stop referring to "the product" and to start realizing once again that they are selling dreams, he wrote, "I could spend a happy holiday on and around Hamstead Heath. . . . The frontier of the dream world is outside the front door."

I read this just after I'd had the same thought during a streetcar ride to a place about five miles from the house where I grew up. If you head south from my home district toward the shore of Lake Ontario, and go across a shipping channel and some railway sidings, past the West Indies Molasses Company, Continental Can, a row of Texico tanks, then over a lift bridge, past Milnes Fuel Oil, Weaver Coal and Warehouse W52, you come out at a place called Cherry Beach, a weedy, willowy strip of sooty shore that lies at the foot of the city like an old abandoned bathing suit. People go there from distant parts of the city, fifteen, twenty miles away. They come from Jaffa, Piraeus and Melbourne, for that matter, for in the evenings seamen from the ships that have come up the St. Lawrence and are unloading or taking on cargo, wander down between the coal piles for a swim.

Except in mid-summer, when the beach becomes crowded and dreadful, it's a quiet, peaceful and strangely exotic place. The swimming is comfortable. The lake water is warmed by the effluent of the Hearn Generating Plant, which returns it at sub-tropical temperatures after it has cooled the boilers, and the city has pronounced that no health hazard is created by the bricks, beer bottles, seaweed, cigarette cartons, pieces of two-by-four, chunks of coal and Coca-Cola cans that glint through the shallow water like coral reefs. Every now and then a green-winged teal with five or six baby ducks floats by.

There are pleasant vistas. You'll see a lone bachelor from one of the nearby rooming-house districts sitting on a crumbling bank, looking out toward the distant dump trucks that roll along the Outer Harbour East Headland, each silhouetted in a haze, like a target in a shooting gallery; not another soul occupies the pleasant prairie of pigweed, plantain and sweet clover that extends between the lone figure and a row of black bunker-fuel tanks. Or you might see a girl in a bikini sitting alone on a blanket that she has spread out for protection from unseen beer tins and popsicle sticks on a sunny, sandy area just south of Liquifuels Limited. She sits there brushing her hair and looking out toward the horizon, as pretty a sight as you'd see in Nice or Monte Carlo.

Cherry Beach lies warm and alive in the imagination of people for whom it once provided hidden corners and nests among the willow groves and coal piles, producing a uniquely disturbing combination of lake, lovers' lane and heavy industry. Today many a middle-

aged man who went to Cherry Beach as a youth can
be maddened by memories of mingled scents of perfume, wet willow leaves and anthracite, and executives
in fifty-seventh-story air-conditioned suites uptown,
who now go to places like Dubrovnik or Buenos Aires
for long week-ends, look out their windows toward the
Milnes Coal Company as if they heard a distant mating
call, their thoughts drifting off to misty nights of long
ago. It's hard to separate the real beach from the one
they remember. Recalling the trees of Cherry Beach, a
man will say, "That was the thickest bush in the world,"
unconscious that he isn't describing a woods, but a
condition of youth.

But the real beach still has a kind of tatty charm,
and the makers of TV commercials and moody docu-
mentaries recognize its mystic qualities. Surprised stroll-
ers have at various times watched an actor rowing
along the shore in a bathtub, exclaiming happily over
somebody's shampoo, a woman folk singer bursting
from an old crumbling lighthouse singing sea chanteys
about somebody's kippers, and even a formal dinner
party being held in a sooty field of weeds. When I was
there last I saw a woman in full bridal costume picking her way daintily through waist-high sweet clover
toward a pile of truck tires, looking like Eustacia Vye
in *The Return of the Native*. It was a restful, mellow
afternoon in October. A lifeguard called languidly,
"Hey, you kids! Quit throwing bricks at the ducks!"
A man in red swim trunks and sunglasses lay asleep
under a low, shimmering poplar, giving the scene a
nice continental touch. At the hot dog stand, a green-
and-red insul-brick-covered building with buckling
pale-green ceiling boards and cottonwood seeds clinging to the roof, the proprietor, a red-haired young man

in frayed blue denim shorts and sandals, leaned over the counter and watched a big, black, fierce-looking German shepherd named Hercules, who was trying to get someone to take an empty beer can from his mouth and toss it for him to retrieve. Along the shore I talked to a man from Poland, who had been sitting by himself in his bathing trunks in a little nest of clothes and blankets, and who got up, pulled on his pants and gave me a short speech about Russia, telling me not to believe anything good I heard about it.

I talked to a couple of friendly drunks, a toothless dishevelled man with a soiled white shirt dangling around his knees, and a red-haired woman who said she wouldn't swim in that water, no matter what the city said, although she *had* taken a dip in it once when she was tight, she said, sitting there in the midst of three dogs, one of which she said was part wolf, and which growled at me. She gave it a thump on the back that made a sound like a drum, then grinned up at me, a diagonal smudge of dust across her lips, which made her look as if she'd been rolled out from under a warehouse. Two kids had made a sand-castle, and drilled a hole down through the top with a soft-drink straw. Now they were pouring some water into it from an old yogurt cup, and watching it run out of some little passageways at the bottom into a moat. A pretty woman with short grey hair picked something up from the sand and told me she was making a collection of water-washed brick and glass. A youngster, fascinated by a floating dead carp, asked me, "Mister, will you get me that fish?" I got it for him. It was the least I could do for a young naturalist.

There was a strong, damp southwest wind rustling the poplars and the seeds were lying around like cotton on a Georgia road. Three excited windblown crows were flapping over a grove of willows. As I headed for the bus that would take me back uptown, the woman who takes care of the bath house and public washrooms waved good-bye and called to me that I really should come down in the evening and see the sunset. She pointed to two towering bank buildings and said it set right between them. She said it was really beautiful—and she said it with more enthusiasm than a lot of tourists I've heard on top of the Acropolis.

The fact is, for the people I'd seen that afternoon, Cherry Beach (which would probably have struck many people as awful) has retained in its gritty way the very essence of travel—the sense of exotic, far-off places, novel sights, the fascination of a beach, and examples of life's little mysteries, like the serene adaptability of green-winged teal to city life. People enjoyed the sun where they found it; looked at the sky through rustling leaves; sought solitude; treasured the feeling of a strange and novel environment; collected beautiful objects, like water-washed bits of beer bottles; and dreamed of the past, when the world was young and full of magic moments like falling in love among the coal piles.

It struck me that if our governments and corporations *do* work things out so that we're back on full-time production of power, and people begin travelling the way they were before the energy crisis, or even faster and oftener, man is going to have to recapture some of the things I saw that day, and develop new techniques to survive the ease and speed of transportation, and the mass annual migrations that have become such big business that they're now listed in government financial reports under Major Items in the Balance on Non-Merchandise Transactions, along with revenue from wood-pulp, crude petroleum and auto parts. He'll need new ideas and he'll have to abandon a lot of old ones.

3

Einstein and the
Herman L. Lily Beauty Salon

One idea that man as tourist will have to get rid of is that if he buys a return ticket to Europe, he's going to be in a perpetual state of sensitive receptivity to cathedrals, monuments, art galleries, museums and beautiful old buildings. It's a great idea, but it doesn't work, which accounts for those gents you see in art galleries, with cameras strapped across their blue windbreakers, yawning in front of oil paintings of dead pheasants, as if wondering, with a kind of horror, if this is really what they've spent their lives promising themselves they'd do some day.

It's a feeling that often comes with doggedly doing the prescribed thing when you're not in the mood for it. It makes more sense to do what one woman I know did. She left a cab with the meter running outside the Louvre, then ran in and out again in twenty minutes so she could say she'd been there (she beat my time by forty minutes).

But there are all kinds of things besides great art for the traveller to see. For instance, these days, when two thirds of the news is about politicians (who are going to have bridges and highways named after them), it can be a fascinating game of detection to try to find memorials and monuments to the world's great thinkers. If you ask about Einstein in Bern, Switzerland, where he worked in a patent office because he wasn't able to get a job teaching physics, you get some reactions that are a lot more educational than looking at medieval carvings on doorways. I can still see the first person I asked about him—a big, handsome girl receptionist in the patent office. She wore a white turtleneck pullover, and had a dimpled chin and a ponytail. She lit a cigarette, blew briskly, frowned at me, shouted "Eh?" at everything I said, told me to sit down, then said something to a tall, politician-like man, who grinned down at me with amusement. Five minutes of this, and you have visions of Einstein coming into the patent office, saying he had come up with this funny equation $E=mc^2$, and whom should he see about it, while the girl in the white sweater shouted, "*Eh?*"

You get a refreshing, first-hand impression of how genius is regarded all over the world, when you mention that you're looking for a memorial to Einstein. People back off and stare at your knees. One Canadian woman tourist shied away from me, went out into the street, looked up at a historic clock set in a carved stone archway and shouted at her husband, who looked as if he wanted to hide, "Somebody did his thing here."

Directions to sites commemorating great thinkers aren't like the directions to the ones commemorating statesmen and soldiers: "It's the second monument on your right past the cathedral," for instance, or, "It's the main statue in the second gallery; the one that nearly touches the ceiling." Tourist-office people, look-

ing rather pleased at your request, tell you to follow a
street till you come to some flowerpots outside a
restaurant, and there's something there about Einstein,
on a post, they think. Taxi drivers steal glances at you
in the rear-view mirror. I told one woman cab driver
with pinkish puffed blond hair that I was looking for
the place where Einstein lived when he was working
out his theory of relativity. She didn't say much but
at the end of the ride we got into a kind of silent
wrestling match over lifting my bag from her trunk,
her own theory of relativity being the principle of
never letting a man get away with anything, even the
idea that he had relatively more muscles than a woman.

There *are* some flowerpots, and an old restaurant
with patched-up, blotchy, pale-green walls, where, the
day I was there, an American woman was shouting, "Do
you think I could get ham and eggs—*no way!*" and
the voice of another woman came booming out of the
WC, "You're in Switzerland!" and a big woman came
out and shouted at a waitress, "We enjoy being here."

The plaque is barely discernible, on a sidewalk pillar.
It says, in German, that Albert Einstein lived in this
house when developing his theory of relativity, and
inside a door beside the restaurant, a narrow, dark stairway leads up to the Herman L. Lily Beauty Salon,
out of which comes a warm breeze of hair lotion, the
fragrance of a mystery deeper than Einstein's concept
of space-time—the Great Women's Hair Mystery. Up
an old peeling spiral staircase there's a mauve door
marked D. Mateo, which I figured was the door to the
apartment Einstein worked in. I knocked but there
was nobody home. (I had hoped I'd find faded little
memos scribbled on the wallpaper like: "There is no

absolute velocity . . . think about this tomorrow after work.") There's another door leading out onto a sunny patch of roof, a nice, drowsy run-down place surrounded by chimney pots, potted plants and peeling yellow plaster walls, with, the day I was there, a washing out on the line—a pair of children's blue denim pants, a napkin, a suit of men's underwear, a shirt, two underwear shorts and one underwear shirt, a red bathing suit—a pink plastic laundry basket and a child's tricycle.

Nearby, in the centre of the street, there's a fountain. In the middle of the fountain is a statue of a bear standing erect wearing a visored helmet, with two swords, a banner and a shield—part of the legend surrounding the founder of Bern, Duke Berchtold of Zähringen, who killed a bear the day of the town's birth, back in 1191. The tourist, reading the inscription and looking at the shields and swords and listening to the water falling, feels that he's back among the warriors and statesmen again. The bear might be pronouncing well-rounded phrases like "I want to make this perfectly clear," or "I have no comment at this present moment of time," and maybe saying something about this great peace-loving country—phrases that make statements like $E=mc^2$ seem like something a bookkeeper would mumble over his soup.

But, speaking for myself, I felt I'd seen something more important than the land staked out by the Duke as I left for Lucerne and my train slid through the farmlands, past emerald green mountains, houses like kitchen clocks, cows, red roofs, geraniums in window boxes, and flowers blowing on railway embankments. I thought of Einstein and Newton and of the first men who tried to figure out the nature of matter, and I thought of the kid who owned the tricycle outside Einstein's old flat, and hoped he was back home safely from school, attaining some satisfying relative velocities of his own.

4

Packaging 2.5 Million Danes

During the past years, just about every magazine you opened showed some guy you didn't particularly want to meet boarding a plane for some place you wanted to keep a private dream until you could afford to go there yourself—and he would be doing it with 385 other people you didn't want to meet. Thanks to the wonders of modern science, there have been threats of planes carrying 4,000 people you don't want to meet, a terrible thought.

Even now travellers are beginning to resent one another. A friend of mine told me that he was with three other men on a canoe trip in the Northwest Territories, a part of Canada so remote and wild that less than 1 per cent has been even surveyed. They had spent three weeks going through desolate, totally uninhabited country, when they met another party, some of whom they knew slightly, going up-river. When my friend told me this I pictured what was coming—bearded men running toward one another along the river bank emitting shouts of joy. But that wasn't what happened. In fact what my friend remembered about the incident, in some awe, was that the parties resented one another, and kept the meeting as short as possible.

I've noticed that people just back from Europe avoid other people just back from Europe, because they don't want to hear them talk about their experiences, or worse, to get invited to see their color slides. For that seems to take the edge off your own adventure; it's rather like driving to your favorite secluded picnic spot and finding three other families already there having supper, or playing softball, or both. With the growing mass migrations of tourists, this has been a factor the tourist has had to cope with, and travel agents have been showing signs of making it worse. A while ago I talked to a happy young agent with brass-colored side-burns who, between phone calls, told me he was working on a new concept, "packaging" countries. "Last year we packaged the Virgin Islands," he said, and went on to say that we're far behind Europe in packaging countries, and that last year Scandinavia packaged 2.5 million Danes, conjuring up visions I'd just as soon forget, and making the travel business sound about as romantic as shipping packaged meats.

But the answer to all this isn't going to be, say, avoiding Europe because *everyone* is going there, but going to someplace in Europe besides cities like Paris and Copenhagen. Thousands of places in every country are never visited by anybody because the places don't show up on the travel folders and have no famous sights. But it's a great experience to drop in on the smallest-looking town on the map, or better still one that doesn't show on a map but which you've seen mentioned in some book on, say, mathematics or languages or history. The people are delighted and surprised that someone found them, and they fix you up little lunches of hard rolls and tomatoes and cheese, and you wander around, the only tourists in town, sometimes getting strange intimations that you've been there before, in another life. You probably know that strange feeling, what the French call *déjà vu*. You're walking across a bridge on a sunny morning when the light glints off the water and seems to turn the very air and grassy banks into pure light, and you see an old graceful dory resting on the water and you stop in your tracks, thinking, "Why, it was on a morning just like this, beside a green field just like that, that I . . ."

On the way to Copenhagen, for instance, tourists pass within thirty miles of the old homeland of the Angles, a group that occupied an angle of land on the Baltic Sea, Angleland, and who gave their name to England, which was then a remote, new, misty lush land of forests they'd found over the sea to the southwest. A visit to a place like that often provides little adventures travel agents have never thought of packaging. If you're as lucky as I was, for instance, you might time things right to ride back to town on a public bus full of school kids, a great way to get a fresh, first-hand vivid feeling for the very roots of Anglo-Saxon history. My wife and I were wedged into the bus among the greatest concentration of tall, good-looking people I've ever seen—kids with hair the color of creamy butter, corn tassels and pure sunlight. We would look along the bus and see, peering through a cluster of a dozen blond heads, a child's face like that of a Swedish movie star, with milk-white skin, pink cheeks and blue eyes, and she would signal and call "sit," meaning it wasn't time for us to get off yet. The whole busload sounded like a flock of geese and smelled as fresh as the sea (with faint overtones of chewing gum), and as we rolled along past fields like green rugs dotted with herds of Holsteins, I got a greater understanding than I ever did at school of the origins of domesticity, exploration, war and coastal raids.

A beautiful schoolgirl with legs that looked long enough for her to walk right over an up-ended meter stick without touching it, reached over and languidly punched a boy. All the boys were punching one another. One plump pink-faced boy sat on a seat near the door and systematically punched each one of his schoolmates as he left the bus, and you knew he was in for a rough day tomorrow, because each one turned, as the doors closed, and gave him a look meaning "I'll punch *you* tomorrow." They were like Holstein bullocks out in the green fields, butting one another for the sheer fun of it.

I remember watching one girl, whose face was a study in relaxed drowsy absorption. She was eating peanuts and listening to what another girl was saying. She'd put a peanut into her mouth, start to bite down on it, then forget it and just look into the face of her girl friend with utter languid concentration, then bite down on the peanut slowly. It was easy to imagine them telling strange tales—about so-and-so's father saying there was a new land out there, and that he was going to sail down the North Sea with his family and a few cattle and move there.

A half-hour like that, and from then on when you read phrases like "a Germanic people" you think of dusk over the broody north European countryside, and feel you're the only tourist to have discovered Europe.

5

Gnawing Your Way Through Europe

Soon, very soon, the world traveller will have to stop going to eating places recommended by tour guides. If they're famous restaurants, becoming more famous as the travel business grows, the tourist will be served by the same hard-boiled bored waiters who serve him in New York or San Francisco, except that they'll speak English with an accent when they explain that the total shown on the bill is "Weethout teep." If they're the other kind of restaurant, recommended for tourists on a low budget, the tourist will have all his meals, including breakfast, with the same stenographer from Detroit with mauve eyelids; she's a nice girl, but you don't need to cross oceans and spend $1,000 to see her.

But the main reason for avoiding these places is that the great experiences of travel, including great eating experiences, are yours alone, and have nothing to do with restaurants picked by other people. It's true that, finding your own food, you'll pick some places that are ghastly, and will find yourself gnawing your way through Europe like a rat, eating stale rolls and hot dogs by green fluorescent lights. But on lucky days you'll strike dining rooms no other tourist ever heard of, patronized by fuddy-duddy well-pickled people who form refreshing little cliques, restful little sociological islands insulated from the lumps and split lips of common life, places with wine-colored walls and delft plates around a rail, and tailcoated waiters who trot toward you if they see you want anything. There'll be just a few other guests—cold-faced elderly women in those German hats with one side of the brim turned down, and silent cold-faced beautiful daughters whose hands have been spoken for and tall cold handsome elderly men with backs like ironing boards—people who think they're better than everybody else (and probably with good reason) and who hate tourists, not the way, say, a New York bus driver hates everyone, but because tourists are intruders into a luxurious privileged world.

They're fascinating to watch. I remember one night my wife and I ducked into a restaurant in a gloomy Gothic hotel somewhere in Germany to get in out of the rain and I spent an hour (incidentally we got a great meal—pork done on a spit, like a shish kebab, with rice in tomato sauce and wonderful smoky-flavored coffee) watching a heavy, sagging bald man with a bare pink face who was ensconced in his corner, which was warmly lit by a table lamp. It was a scene of pure, unabashed, voluptuous indulgence. He didn't exactly order his meal. He and the waiter quietly raped the menu, chuckling and murmuring together, the man putting his nose right down on the menu like an old beagle sniffing good things. He never looked at the waiter. They just entered into a familiar conspiracy, the man tracing out the items with his forefinger and keeping up a growling commentary. When he tasted the wine, you knew he really tasted it, and thought

about it, the way, say, a skilled mechanic might listen
to a Rolls-Royce engine.

This is something that we North Americans never
quite pull off, no matter how hard we try. It's especially
tough for people like me, who came from districts
where wine was something drunk at night by nomadic
characters who had soirées late Saturday night and
drifted on, leaving their empty bottles in people's gera-
nium beds. No matter how often I smell the cork and
take sips and say, "That's fine," when paid actors pour
little bits into my glass for me to taste, to prove I'm
not trying to poison my guests, it's a self-conscious,
ridiculous little ritual that always makes me blush. But
this guy went at it as naturally as my father would
have gone at a job of plumbing. I've never seen anyone so much at home in a restaurant. It was a world
where he growled or raised a finger and people brought
things to him and took things away.

Even when you miss a place like this, little things
happen that don't happen in internationally famous
restaurants where your roast beef order is sliced at
your table by a duke's cousin. I can still see a plump
little woman in a brown coat who, one night when I
was trying to get some food out of a machine in the
basement of a big gloomy railway station, came up,
put a coin in, handed me a paper cup of hot, vile coffee, and refused to take any money from me, saying
after carefully thinking out the English words, "You
are the guest of France," as delightful and formal a
little bit of protocol as I've ever seen. And I remember
another time in the railway station restaurant in Lyons.
It was jammed with people going to work mingling
with people who had been up all night. The floor was
littered, people were lined up three deep at the bar,

and some people were taking food after a long night, catching their breath, licking their wounds. There were crumbs on the tables, and spilled wine. I'd been trying unsuccessfully to get a drink of water from baffled waiters—not mineral water, not water with the gas, not water natural, WATER—like well, WATER—and was beginning to feel wretched and homesick when a business girl, who was having an early morning coffee at the next table, told the waiter what I wanted, moved back her chair, got up and smiled at my wife and me, and on an impulse reached over and put her container of jam, which she hadn't used, in front of us—an oddly friendly domestic gesture, suggesting real people with things in the refrigerator and late night snacks. It completely removed my mood of homesickness, something that wouldn't have happened in the most famous restaurants in Europe.

6

Homesickness

Homesickness is something people will have to learn to deal with as travel becomes an accepted way of life, and people start to feel almost forced to go to some place other than the one they're in, so as not to be out of the mainstream of human progress. Yet some people never get over homesickness.

Once, on a train from Zurich to Geneva, I sat next to a man from Patras, who took out a tape recorder, rubbed it lovingly with a piece of cloth, then played a tape of himself singing, accompanied by a bouzouki, two bars over and over again for about half an hour until a Swiss soldier stood up and shouted at him, making furious gestures, as if getting water out of his ears, and the Greek put the tape recorder back in his bag. I felt sorry for the guy. He was just homesick, and I think everyone there felt guilty as hell when he wrapped the thing up and put it away. He turned to me and apologized for not letting me hear more of it, but indicated that the other people didn't like it, which made me feel even worse than the others, because I didn't like it either. Nobody said good-bye to him when they left him sitting there—a new kind of man—away from home, displaced, bewildered, not rich, among strangers, moving through a prim green Swiss countryside dotted with neat little farms that looked as if their owners would flog you with wet oak leaves if you had an immortal idea; dreaming of his sunny, crumbling land, falling apart and friendly. He disappeared into a fine, cold rain at a little town near Olten. I don't know where he went or why he went there, but I hope he found a snug fireplace with ten people playing the bouzouki and lots of ouzo.

It's not only the unsophisticated who get homesick. I came across a pretty blond young seasoned traveller in shorts standing in a phone booth in Rome sobbing, thoroughly homesick for Paris. We found this out when my wife went over and talked to her and, with a gush of relieved feelings, the girl told her that last night she had been slapped, felt, fondled and followed until her nerves had snapped and she had been trying to phone her father, a doctor in Paris, just to hear his voice, and when she couldn't get him she just started crying. She stood talking to us gratefully—if for no other reason than that for a moment she had someone protecting her from attack from the rear.

In the American Express office in Nice I watched a tall, homely American girl who was dressed in blue jeans, red head scarf and sandals, and carried a knapsack and duffel bag—the picture of blasé, world-travelled youth—ask for mail, only to find that there was none for her. She turned around and said to the world in general, "I—have—had—it!" Her face started to kind of swell and get soft, and I realized that she was crying. The girl behind the mail counter in this town, which is in the very heart of the Riviera, where the happy traveller is supposed to be always running after someone in a bikini, or being chased into the sea by someone with hair on his chest, told me that the only thing she didn't like about her job was watching people, mostly girls, cry when there was no mail for them. Homesick men acted differently, she said. They got mad and yelled at her. Sometimes people who got mail sat right down and read the letters, laughing and crying and reading parts aloud. "Hey! Listen to this. Dad fell over the lawnmower on Saturday!" Sometimes the American Express girl, who is supposed to preserve a strict official secrecy, gets so involved that she calls out happily to someone she has seen come in for mail for a week, "There's a letter from Mary for you."

It seems to me that the airlines of the future will miss a bet if they don't take into account the homesick tourist. They could have a special kind of stewardess who, instead of wearing a uniform, would wear a frumpy, homely polka-dot dress, and there would be one steward in a green cardigan and carpet slippers who would pull up a chair, put his feet on a portable imitation wood-stove that could be wheeled down the aisle with the whiskey cart, and chat about things like woodchucks and western sandwiches, and assure the homesick tourist that three weeks would soon be over and he would be back home again before he knew it.

In the meantime, tourists will feel less self-conscious about being homesick, if they can mingle with Italians, who get so homesick they just about turn travel into an opera, wandering around airports and ports of disembarkation red-eyed and distraught. Men with hardlined faces look right through you with tears pouring down their cheeks. When a boat leaves Genoa, a wailing rises from both the pier and the boat that just about drowns out the ship's horn.

Watching an Italian flight departure is something

that will make any homesick tourist of the future feel a lot better about being homesick himself. I remember watching a CP Air flight on which a lot of grandparents who had been visiting their Canadian-based families and grandchildren, were going home, and it was an experience that took the onlookers right back to the beginnings of man. Two homely little gnomes of women with red, wet, puckered faces clung to one another until I found myself hoping the plane wouldn't be able to take off. Younger women stared into space, very carefully not crying, but you knew that if you shook them, the tears would fall like ripe Mediterranean olives. Women were dragged to the departure lounge, heads lolling in despair. Husbands supported wives. Friends tried to rescue friends from the awful fate of going somewhere away from their families.

Some made touching efforts to be as cold as an old Anglo-Saxon Torontonian. A dapper, moustached, middle-aged man in a natty mustard-colored hat looked cynical and exasperated by all this display of emotion, then suddenly buried his face in a handkerchief, pressing it to his face with both hands. A fashionable woman in purple cork-soled sandals, purple pants and rust-colored shaggy coat, laughed and threw kisses merrily, until she suddenly clapped her hand over her face like an oxygen mask, and you knew this frigid land wasn't hers. There were smacking sounds of men kissing grandmothers, grandmothers kissing babies, men kissing men, men kissing women. A great wailing sound arose from the group. People faced one another in circles, all crying and looking at their toes. Teen-age girls cried. I started to cry. I knew what they were going through; I get homesick if I go from Toronto

to Ottawa, a distance of 250 miles. A CP Air stewardess worked her way through the crowd, muttering
through tight lips, "Jesus!" There were horrendous
screams. Everyone surged to see someone even un-
happier than they were. A blond woman shouted as if
she had her foot in a trap. Then everyone went out to
watch the big DC-8 that was screaming and gliding
through the night like a great orange and silver lizard.

A lot of our standard beliefs don't jibe with reality,
and one of them is that travellers are always carefree
and happy, and that there are places in this world,
usually associated with bathing and sunshine, where
everybody is automatically delirious with joy. All of
this is supported by thousands of travel ads. A recent
one shows a woman at the kitchen sink laughing so
hard her eyes are closed because her husband apparently sneaked up behind her, tickled her and shouted
"We're off to Amsterdam!"

It reminded me of a brisk, businesslike girl with a
red umbrella who took time out on her way to night
school in Amsterdam to show my wife and me some of
her city, stepping along smartly, like a small soldier,
opening a wooden gate in a wall and taking us into a
beautiful, hidden circle of houses, and pointing out
step houses and clock houses with her red umbrella,
and every time we protested that she was making herself late for night school, saying, "Please! Never mind!"
But what I remember most was her feelings about her
home town. She said she'd been to other cities of the
world, but there was nothing like Amsterdam. She'd
never leave it. She never wanted to live anywhere else,
or even go anywhere else.

I've never seen anyone who was so glad she wasn't
travelling anywhere, except my father and the other

people of the street where I grew up. Homesickness was a normal part of life in my neighborhood. None of us could stand being away from home very long. My own family handed down a tradition of homesickness from generation to generation, like the family china. My grandparents moved to Vancouver once, but stayed only two days, partly because their dog, a pug named Buddy, died, probably from homesickness. My father made one trip as a young man, to Boston, which at the age of ninety-five he still cited as an example of the horrors of leaving home, having undergone a kind of metaphysical bends at finding that nothing really changes with travel, except to get worse. As long as I knew him he never wandered much further away from home than downtown.

My mother stayed away from home only once that I know of, when she stayed overnight with friends on a farm seven miles out of the city. That night she looked out of her window during a storm, when the lightning lit up the tombstones in a country churchyard nearby. She came home bright and early next day and didn't stop talking for a week.

My older brother, a precise and formal youth, put his hat on firmly one time and went to Kansas City, but he was the only wanderer among all the kids on the block. We took long Saturday bike rides into strange parts of town, riding over streetcar cobbles with creaking sprockets and rattling fenders, past such strange sights as looming gas tanks and factories that dribbled steam and water over sooty brick walls, but we'd all be back in time for supper, wrestling with the dog, lifting the lids off saucepans, beaming contentedly when our mothers rapped us over the head, through with travel for a week at least. After my family got a car, a Model

T Ford sedan, and began going for drives, I used to ask when we were going home soon after we started, exasperating even my father, who was having enough trouble driving, which he never completely mastered.

I still think of the girl in Amsterdam sometimes, especially when I'm poised for flight, passport in order, vaccination itching, part of me looking forward to the great adventure of seeing far-off, exotic lands, part of me remembering the unpleasant feeling of being a foreigner, of mingling with people who don't know me and don't want to know me, and wishing I could sell my ticket and call the whole thing off. Yet coping with homesickness is one of the techniques that will have to be acquired by the tourist, since this generation is moving around at a greater rate than man has moved at any time in history. He's going to have to learn that homesickness is an important part of travel. It has nothing to do with what's going on outside him, but it has a lot to do with what's going on inside him—one of the last unexplored regions left for the tourist.

7

"*Have You Read* War and Peace?"
"*No, But I've Been to Leningrad.*"

Soon, we're told, we'll have super aircraft that will
carry us across the Atlantic at a cost per passenger comparable to a bus fare from New York to San Francisco,
a triumph of technology that should result, before long,
in everybody in the world having been everywhere, at
least once. We're going to have to start all over again
with a new approach to travel: for instance, once more
making travel a sort of supplement to reading, a pas-
time that has fallen off in inverse proportion to the
speed of jets. It's easy to see why. It's easier to fly to
Rome than to read Gibbon's *Decline and Fall of the
Roman Empire*, and a lot faster, and you don't have to
sit still or stop talking while you're doing it. Further-
more, when someone asks, for instance, "Have you read
War and Peace?" and you can say, "No, but I've been
to Leningrad," it combines the pleasure of being knowl-
edgeable without reading and the joy of clobbering
someone. Another thing, travel is less discouraging than
trying to find books in those modern book departments
where all the titles you want are hidden either in
glassed-in cupboards, like those dishes nobody used
that were displayed on Victorian plate rails, or in

drawers beneath displays of hot-water bottles, and all you can find are forty-five-dollar books of photographs as big as doorsteps, and sales bins of ghosted autobiographies like *My Ten Wasted Years as a Virgin* or publishers' remainders of books with weird titles like *How to Clean Shotguns.*

Yet to the romantic, the great moments of travel share the same magic as that created by great writers. I don't mean writers of those tour books that describe countries with a bouncy enthusiasm that makes you vow never to go there, with readers' notes like "Alice and I found a charming little rooming house in Jerusalem run by three football players from Atlanta." I mean writers like Thomas Hardy, who give villages and countrysides another kind of life and existence. The very stones of buildings come to life as you stand there remembering scenes like the one where Hardy describes a dandelion seed floating down the middle of the main street, from one end to the other, and out into the country again, and you relive his stories of a still, quiet world of dairy herds, hayricks, grainfields and women as warm and simple as new laid eggs.

One of the great travel experiences for me was visiting Dorchester and stepping into that solid stone geometrical, prim, countryfied formal setting where through Hardy I had lived through so many dramatic events involving all the main issues that still torment mankind—marriage, love, sex, dreams of success, failure. I had never read a biography of Hardy and knew nothing about the real settings for his novels, and I found it as exciting as a trip in a time machine to discover them. One time I asked someone where I could find a good hotel and was told to go to one with a name I'd never heard of. I had a cup of coffee, then wan-

dered upstairs to a big empty unlit TV lounge and
went over to the window and looked down at the street
and realized, thanks to Hardy's genius for giving the
very feeling of a place, that I was looking out the window he had described in the story (based on fact) of
a man named Henchard, who sold his wife to a sailor,
one night when he was drunk at a country fair. For a
moment there I saw Henchard's former wife, standing on her toes, looking in through the window (*my*
window), trying to get a look at Henchard, her husband of long ago, who was now the Mayor of Caster-
bridge.

Reading switches on some kind of live current between the tourist and the place he's visiting. One time
I drove around the awful polluted ship canals and riv-
ers and industrial jungles around Chicago; I was looking for a canoe route. I'd been reading Francis Park-
man's wonderful books about the French exploration
of North America and I found myself asking directions
as if Chicago were still solid forest, startling service-
station attendants with questions about canoe routes.
"You're looking for *what?*" "An Indian portage," I'd
say. "La Salle used it."

La Salle, a neurotic, humorless iron man with shoul-
der-length locks, dismissed an epic tangle of debts with
one of history's great understatements: "I have neither
the habit nor the inclination to keep books." He travelled by birchbark canoe from Montreal to what is now
the site of New Orleans, and back. His route (to use
names of present places as reference) took him up the
St. Lawrence to Kingston, Ontario, along the north
shore of Lake Ontario to Toronto, up the Humber
River, over a portage, down the Holland River into
Lake Simcoe, up to Lake Couchiching at the north end

of Lake Simcoe, down the Severn River to Georgian
Bay, north through the pink granite islands that lie like
a lace fringe along the shore, some so low that a great
blue heron standing on one has his feet awash, and so
into Lake Huron, past Manitoulin, through the Straits
of Mackinac, down Lake Michigan to Benton Harbor,
over to the west side of Lake Michigan, up the Chicago
River, along the south fork, up a north branch of the
south fork, and over a portage across a low divide to
the Des Plaines River and down this to the Illinois and
on to the Mississippi.

The Chicago portage was a main point for the forest
travellers of that day since it lay between waters that
flowed into the North Atlantic and waters that flowed
into the Caribbean. The east end of the old Chicago
portage is buried now beneath the city, but the west
end, although it lies amid Standard Oil tanks near a
traffic sign that says, "Use headlights through the
smoke," is surrounded by a surprisingly pretty little
wooded park, or was the last time I was there. I found
it one sunny morning in late summer. As I followed a
trail down to a pond, the sound of the traffic disappeared. The woods became as silent as they were when
La Salle went through here (a lot more silent, in fact,
as he was accompanied by twenty-three Frenchmen,
eighteen New England Indians, ten Indian women and
three children). I skirted the pond, came to another
trail and began a gradual ascent past a concrete culvert; when I reached the top, before me I saw the Des
Plaines, just as La Salle and his company had found it,
gurgling along peacefully at the foot of the slope, its
waters on the way to the savannas and saw grass of
the Gulf of Mexico, where La Salle was later murdered
by his men.

On my way I had passed a big rock that had obviously once had a plaque inserted in its face. I counted thirty-three beer tins but no plaque, and when I got back to the highway, I went to a phone booth at a filling station and called the Chicago Historical Society. Amid the roar of passing trucks came a faint cultured, surprised voice, that said, "Just a moment, please," and I had a feeling that the operator had switched me back to the seventeenth century and put me through to a Jesuit mission and that the owner of the voice was shuffling down a dim hall that smelled faintly of onion soup. The man came back on the line and told me that I had indeed been standing at the west end of the Chicago portage, and that there had been a plaque on the rock giving this information. The plaque had been stolen during World War II, and replaced in 1947, and I was the first to break the news that it had been stolen again. Nobody before or since has been more satisfied than I was that day with a trip to Chicago.

Reading, and recollections of past reading, can add a lot to travel. This applies even on sight-seeing tours, if you can get away from the guides. Ernest Hemingway's home in Key West has a nice big square bathroom with the sun coming in low over a red tile floor, and standing looking in the door you can picture Hemingway lying there in the big tub composing lines like "There were chimney swifts in the sky. After a while it got dark and the searchlights came on." In Bath, in the west of England, you can sit drinking coffee in the Pump Room listening to a string orchestra half hidden by date palms, chrysanthemums and poinsettias, picturing Henry Fielding sitting there working out his characters for *Tom Jones*, one of whom, Squire Allworthy, was patterned after a prominent citizen of

Bath. Other people who lived in Bath at one time or
another, were Clive of India, Dr. Livingstone, Gains-
borough, Dickens, Goldsmith, Nelson, Jane Austen and
General Wolfe (who was living there when he got his
order to sail to capture Quebec). As you sit there, listening to the genteel orchestra, you have thoughts of
another of Fielding's characters, Sophia Western's father, roaring onto the scene with one of his prize pigs
and falling, and his sister leaning over him saying,
"Get up! You country clot!"

Apart from the close connection between reading
and travel, looking for books can be even more fun
than looking for old plaques. Today the phrase "browsing through bookstores," has a sad little ring, like the
sound of a clavichord, yet a revival of the thought
would open up great new travel possibilities for a lot of
people. In some cities books and reading are still part
of the very feeling of the place. In San Francisco, where
roof-sitting is a fine, civilized local custom, people sit
reading on top of apartment buildings amid a fine lu-
minescent mist and the lament of fog horns, and there
are more second-hand bookstores there, or seem to be,
than in any other place in North America. My own
theory about this is that people pour into California
weekly, intending to stay there for life, pulling U-Haul
trailers full of their household possessions, including
books, and that the books either get left behind when
they move somewhere else, or get stolen and re-dis-
tributed.

I contributed to the books of San Francisco myself
once when San Franciscans robbed my car of everything I owned, and I've often had visions since of
groups of young people sitting around on water beds,
smoking hookahs and puzzling over some of the papers

I was carrying like "The Incidence of Pregnancy of Moose in Newfoundland." Kids come to San Francisco having broken all ties with their homes and childhood, but secretly they have packed a few sentimental keepsakes, like disintegrating copies of *Anne of Green Gables*, awarded for Sunday-school attendance and signed by aunts, and eventually the books turn up on the shelves of Goodwill stores, along with Brown Betty teapots and stone bed warmers from the T. Eaton Company and second-hand toasters, and it's great fun discovering old titles you've almost forgotten, especially when a certain zest and interest is added by the surroundings.

You can stand in a second-hand bookstore on a drowsy spring afternoon, the smell of hamburgers coming in the open door, reading lines like "One sunshiny morning in June, there drove up to the great iron gate of Miss Pinkerton's academy for young ladies, on Chiswick Mall . . ." while listening to the faint cries of front men proclaiming stark, raw, naked, topless, bottomless sex. Or maybe you come across an old Boy Scout handbook in a store down on Market Street, and you turn to those familiar, hearty bits of advice like "In order to get money, fellows must expect to work," while outside the door old-time panhandlers in frayed zoot suits are picking up butts or some brisk young fellow is stopping passers-by with "Pardon me, sir. Could you spare a dollar? This is my birthday."

There used to be fascinating debates continually going on in one store I liked on Polk Street, where they served customers coffee at a tatty counter beside the cash register while I moused around the shelves finding books I hadn't seen since I was a kid. I remember once finding Thornton W. Burgess' *Animal Book* and

going over all the familiar old color plates of woodchucks and weasels while listening to a debate going
on at the counter about whether a $150 prostitute was
as immoral as a ten-dollar prostitute, a fine point that
would have baffled Old Mother West Wind.

The last time I was in San Francisco there was a sale
of tens of thousands of used books in a huge building
down by Civic Center. The books were arranged in
rows beneath naked electric bulbs along long, shaky
plank tables. Watching the crowd around the tables,
I got the distinct feeling that real book people were already beginning to look a bit like whooping cranes and
other threatened species. They dived into the books
eagerly, got their hair into them, looked as if they were
going to eat them. One rumpled book-man with thick
glasses ran a finger over the pages, chuckling over a
paragraph here and there, unconscious of the long,
curved ash of his cigarette dropping down the front of
his pants. Book people going different ways down the
stacks of books did courtly little minuets to get past
one another. They stood, a book in each hand, looking
indecisive, or they dragged fingers affectionately over
the backs as they drifted down the aisles, as if floating
slowly downstream in canoes. Family groups squatted
cross-legged on the floor beside stacks of books they'd
chosen, like Plains Indians. A Chinese girl fondled *The
Understanding Heart* by Peter B. Kyne, looking as if
she might sit beside an arched painted bridge composing those airy verses like "If a small boy serves tea
beside a willow on a cloudy day, is not this better than
an itchy back?"

The non-book people looked as if they didn't belong
there. They tended to rear back when they looked at
books, and they turned the pages at arm's length, dis-

approvingly, clipping the pages as if they were inter-
rogating someone. They stood with their hands behind
their backs, not touching the books, looking as if they
were slapping their leggings with riot sticks, making
notes of titles dangerous to public morals. Some read
books furtively, holding them down at hip level, like
Wyatt Earp sneaking a look at his watch to see if Doc
Holliday was due for his duel. A boy holding a taffy
apple picked up a paperback horror story in his free
hand, dangled it the way he might hold a broken
hockey stick, and said to his mother without looking
at her, "Here." His mother looked at the book, said,
"Okay," and dropped it into a box. One boy all the
time I was there stood drumming out a military march
on a cardboard carton of the Encyclopaedia Britannica.
When a bored baby, in one of those little knapsacks
that young mothers use, let out a scream, people froze
with books in their hands, as if in some future world
they'd been caught reading by Number Two.

Young lovers were divided by their attitudes toward
books. A girl in blue jeans said wistfully to her boy-
friend, who walked swiftly past all the books, not even
noticing the titles, "I just wish you'd *read* some of
them."

Then suddenly a frenzy came over everyone. A man
in a pink-striped shirt called out, his voice sounding
oddly human and alive (because, I realized afterward,
he didn't use a microphone), "All books from now until
closing, one dollar a carton."

It was as if The Day had arrived—the last chance
for mankind to make up its mind whether it wanted
books or not before the lights went out. There was a
rush for empty boxes. A woman snapped three from
under my nose. Everyone panicked trying to find books

they had previously passed up. They called out to one another. "How much room have we got left in the box?" The young man who had walked past all the books was now tossing everything into his box, like provisions. His girl friend said, "For Pete's sake, take something you want to *read!*"

I got *The Forsyte Saga* by Galsworthy, a book by Alexander Woollcott, *The Cloister and the Hearth, Tono-Bungay,* a history of England, and, by a stroke of luck, found a book which I had glanced at earlier and knew contained an essay called "On the Scope and Nature of University Education" by Cardinal John Henry Newman which said: "The university student profits by an intellectual tradition. . . . a habit of mind . . . which lasts through life, of which the attributes are freedom, equitableness, calmness, moderation and wisdom." The warehouse was getting dim. We all left, as the lights went out one by one, marching with cartons on our heads, into God knows what kind of a future.

8

Nomads in California

Aside from its association with old books, California has played a big part in the lives of my wife and myself. Early in our married life, we began talking about the weather and the perfect climate and ideal place to live, and we kept it up well into young parenthood. Every few years during a blizzard we'd decide to go to California, or, sometimes, Florida, and several times both. We drove between California and Florida so often that eventually we wouldn't even bother to pick up road maps when we set out. We'd occasionally come to a dead halt on a strange road, with the radiator up against somebody's livestock pens, but by and large we got to know the route like commuters. We often spent Christmas in motels, for Christmas in the North, or the week before, is the best time to start moving to California. We rigged up Christmas trees of sagebrush for the kids in the back seat of the car, had lunches, watched by little lizards, in scrubby canyons that had the feeling of going back to the time when the earth's crust was beginning to cool, and sang Christmas carols driving beneath moonlit desert peaks, headed for the night's stop at some place like Alpine, or Searchlight or Twentynine Palms.

For periods ranging from a few months to a year, we *did* live in California. We lived in Laguna Beach and Santa Ana and West Los Angeles and Needles and San Francisco. There's no question about it, California has the ideal climate (assuming the ideal is moderate temperatures, sunshine and no snow except in the mountains) with few bugs and rarely high humidity, and probably more beautiful country than any other area in the United States or Canada. Laguna Beach, with which I'll always associate a fragrance of char-boiled steaks, eucalyptus trees, kelp, mist and sun-tan lotion, is set between rolling green hills and a rocky shore, with tidal pools like little aquariums in which you can see sea anemones and crabs and occasionally a small octopus. Seals come up onto the beach now and then, and sometimes you can see whales spouting about halfway to the horizon. I spent hundreds of hours climbing around the rocks, never without getting soaked, as the Pacific Ocean is deceptive. You'll be looking out at a calm and peaceful sea, and realize suddenly that the whole horizon is rising and that it's a big wave coming in, and start clambering. But it always manages, somehow, to catch you and slip around behind your feet, with an eerie accompaniment of air being compressed in subterranean caves, making moaning sounds.

In California, the desert is within a half a day's drive or less. Even Los Angeles has its charms. In spite of the fact that everything bad that the automobile has done to modern life took place there, with freeways over freeways over freeways, there are calm and sunny palm-decorated neighborhoods, and you don't have to drive too far to be in open rangeland. Oddly, one of the longest, most deserted stretches I've ever driven

while running short of gas was on Route 5 north of Los
Angeles. It's not a wilderness like, say, the stretch in
Northern Ontario between Hearst and Longlac; but
it's a lonely region of endless rolling green hills that
gives you an eerie feeling when the gas tank is low,
like somebody who won't stop smiling at you. Farther
north, toward San Francisco, there are some of the
world's most spectacular meeting places of land and
water. Around the Monterey Peninsula and Big Sur
you can come out on stretches of beach through an
archway in the rocks, and look out at a scene that is
just the way it looked to the Spanish explorers, or Sir
Francis Drake, who sailed right past San Francisco
Bay without seeing it.

Yet we never stayed in California. My wife and I,
on cold mornings, still argue about whether it was just
I who wanted to leave, or both of us; we each claim it
was the other one's idea. Probably the reason was that
for someone from northeast North America it's just too
drastic a change, and we shied away from it, the way
someone might dig his heels in if he found himself actually being hauled through the gates of heaven. At
any rate, we didn't stay, and for years we've often
talked about the time when we went mad, periodically
selling everything we owned, including our house, and
heading for California, ending up broke, displaced and
desperate for money, with me having to write and sell
something by next Friday to pay expenses for the next
couple of weeks.

We talked about it with fond little smiles, as something in our past, something that happened in our early
years of precarious finances, until a few years ago a
strange thing happened. We decided to do it again.

Within a couple of months we had moved out of our apartment, sold our furniture, put a few things in storage, and headed for San Francisco. For one thing, we wanted to be closer to our daughters and one son-in-law who were now living there. We intended to find a modest place to rent, but weren't able to, and we knew that moving in with our kids, which was what they wanted us to do, was not the right answer.

So one morning we found ourselves parked in a supermarket lot south of San Francisco eating a sandwich lunch made on the road, looking out over the Pacific, without the faintest idea where we were going to live. It gradually dawned on us that once more we were without a home and had no place to go. What was worse, we were unable to decide what to do, whether to turn back and head for Florida, or Canada, or go south to San Diego, or Mexico, or turn east to Needles. It was like waking up in a dream, not exactly a nightmare, but one with a highly nervous quality. We were both not only middle-aged, but on the brink of senior citizenship, and here we were homeless again and rapidly going broke. Every half-hour or so, we'd drive out of the parking lot and take a little trip down the coast highway, instinctively feeling that moving pavement and scenery would somehow provide solutions. Then we'd come back and look at the sea and have another sandwich. Or my wife, trying to dispel the feeling of unreality, would say, "We'll have to buy a teapot."

We did get a place eventually, but later found out that during this bad period our daughters had been looking at those public service announcements on TV that ask, "Do you know where your children are tonight?" thinking, "Do *you* know where your parents

are tonight?" We left at the end of six months, wondering if we should have stayed. The moral here is that too
much travelling can put people in strange, stressful
situations.

9

"Champlain?
You Better Ask in the Office."

There's still a lingering conviction that travel is educational, but with the vast swarms of other tourists we have to contend with, the educational side of it means less and less. Standing at Versailles, making notes, or, worse still, taking pictures, with 200 other tourists from Cleveland and Sioux City gives you no more feeling of the past than dropping in to a Rexall drugstore.

Still, today's fast-moving tourist can arrange his own history lessons, by getting away from the main tourist centres. He can relive some of the episodes of the past —at least in feeling. He can do it, even, by utilizing modern conveniences. Once I took a cab from Rochefort to the birthplace of Champlain, and let the cab go. It was something like being shot back 360 years in a space capsule. Champlain was one of the truly great figures in North American history. He didn't barge around through the bush seeing how far he could go, but based his activities around the St. Lawrence and when he did travel, up around Georgian Bay, he made careful observations of the tribal customs of the Tobacco Indians. Some of these notes still read like an account of a visit today to Grand Bend, a beach resort where young people from the United States and Canada gather on Labour Day to drink, parade in bikinis, dance, make love and pack the cabins until it's hard to tell who's keeping house in whose wigwam. In 1615 Champlain wrote, "When night comes, the young women run from one cabin to another, as do the young men on their part, visiting any girls they please—they incur no ill repute or insult for it for it is the custom of the country."

As a school kid I used to like to read of the adventures of Champlain and the Order of Bon Temps that his company formed during his first winter on the island of St. Croix in the mouth of the St. John River in New Brunswick, which was illustrated in my history book by drawings of smiling men in pantaloons carrying platters of roast duck. I don't know how kids feel about Champlain today. A while ago I asked a youngster who was sitting on the floor in a school corridor if he knew who Champlain was, and he said, "*Who* you looking for?" "Champlain." "You better ask in the office," he said. "*They'll* know who he is." He probably figured I was looking for some kid who'd let the air out of my tires—some fresh kid named Jimmy Champlain.

When I visited Champlain's birthplace, in Brittany, I began to get into the mood of the days when wooden sailing ships were heading out for the Americas, just as soon as my cab left me standing in the middle of the village of Brouage. Today it is a grim little place of crumbling stone and plaster, surrounded by flat marshlands and lime-green canals, with ramparts and lookouts and a billion flies of a kind I've never seen before. But that night I joined an order of *bon temps* myself.

I met the mayor, a boisterous man in a red sweater

coat, who came out at the sight of a real live tourist in town. He mentioned Champlain's astrolabe, the brass navigation instrument Champlain lost near the Ottawa River in 1613 and which was found by a schoolboy 254 years later, in 1867. He took me to the village tourist bureau, a cheerless stone building, to show the astrolabe to me, and it turned out to be a copy presented to Brouage by Computing Devices of Canada Limited; the real one is in New York City, in the Museum of the New York Historic Society.

There was no hotel in Brouage. The mayor drove me to the neighboring village of Hiers and left me to spend the night in a scuffed little combination hotel, bar and restaurant, as rough as a cabin on St. Croix. Half a dozen farmers and oyster fishermen were shouting and dropping bags of walnuts and making noisy jokes. One man, who looked like a cat, began meowing and put his foot up on a table, and, amid great hilarity, another man pulled the cat's shoes off and threw them at the door. They all gave a rousing cheer when the woman who ran the place led me upstairs to my bedroom. She turned and grinned at me in a kind of fond apology for her friends below, opened the door to a room with an unpainted board floor, a cowskin rug (Hereford), a bidet and a cloud of flies around the ceiling light. She opened the window and showed me where the sea was, three miles away, and some lights on a distant bridge, and told me to come down for supper in half an hour.

It was all rough, simple and convivial. The dining area of the bar had the decor of a half-finished garage, but the big history lesson for me was my meal (I was the only diner). It was served with grace, style and the courtly manner that the French must have observed back in those early days in the wilds of North America, and which is about as extinct in middle-class English-speaking America today as the passenger pigeon—napkin in a silver holder, gleaming white tablecloth, more silverware than I knew how to use, big soup tureen, a basket of fruit, a vase of flowers. The food was better than any I've ever had in a three-decker North American motel with an acre of broadloomed lobby, and the company was a lot more genuinely hospitable. The men at the bar made great efforts to make it clear that I was welcome. When, after a five-minute exchange of words, I got across that I wanted a drink of water, a man in a beret said, "Ahhhhh!" as if the mystery were solved at last and apologized to me, then toasted me. We clinked glasses. Another man came over and shook hands with me and wished me *bon appétit.* The woman wished me *bon appétit.* A stocky man in braces behind the bar toasted me and then toasted Champlain, then Canada, and wished us all a *bon appétit,* and the feeling in the room, I was convinced, was the same as that in that log cabin three hundred and fifty years ago.

I went for a stroll that evening in a village that sounded the way the North American bush must have sounded in Champlain's day. I'd forgotten what the silence of a village was like before transistor radios, television, outboards and snowmobiles. I could hear my own footsteps. I could hear the blood in my ears. I could hear the town hall clock whirring *before* it struck. Some ducks let out a boisterous laugh in the dark. A cat came out of a stone house with a mouse in its mouth and froze at the sight of me. I looked up at the Big Dipper, the pointers right then pointing to North America, and wondered what thoughts Champlain had as a young man as he looked out in the same direction from this region of quiet farmland and salt marshes, as he pondered the shape of North America, which in those days was more of an enigma than the surface of the moon today.

10

Sitting Still for Three Weeks

There's nothing wrong with those three-week vacations made possible by today's air travel, which cover everything in ten countries from the Blarney stone to the Temple of Poseidon; but the tourist should keep in mind (in fact, he'll *have* to keep it in mind if he's going to retain the joy of travel) that a trip like that doesn't result in your seeing Europe, or any other place. He can do the whole thing all over ten times in a novel way, for instance, by going to each place again and *sitting still* for three weeks. The traveller is often on a tighter schedule than he's on back at work, where he can at least take long lunch hours and lots of coffee breaks. If you take a coffee break on some of those tours, where you hear people saying things like "We go to the Acropolis this morning and Sounion this afternoon and we'll be back in Houston on Saturday," you'll miss something, like 2,000 years of history.

But there's no better way of seeing a country than finding some obscure corner, sitting down as unobtrusively as possible, and just watching the people and letting their customs and history soak in.

Greece, a country where tourists exhaust themselves more than in any other, clambering over the sites of

man's past, is designed for sitting still. You can still sit
outside taverns that will inspire you to ponder, like
Socrates, eternal questions like "What is The Good?"
as you look around at surroundings that look like a
demolition site, with plaster dust poured over it, everything needing fixing—crumbling stone walls, broken
bricks, dry baked dirt lanes, broken flagstone sidewalks,
leaning sidewalk tables and maybe a lone Greek sitting
having coffee in the tremendous heat, with the bright
sun making little short shadows and a hot, dry wind
carrying the smells of olive oil, Papastratos cigarettes,
and braised corn—and you suddenly realize with a
mild, philosophical shock that you love the place and
never felt better, and you wonder what you were trying
to accomplish at home all those Saturdays of plumbing
and painting and cutting lawns and fixing things.

All Greek villages have central squares where the
whole population comes in the evening, to stroll and
sit at tables that extend as far as you can see beneath
the trees, and where you can hear low voices and
laughter, the sounds of kids playing, and the scuff of
strolling feet, and watch the parade of posh baby car-
riages, and reflect on the passage of time and the suc-
cession of generations.

I remember sitting in the square at Heraklion one
evening when a brass band arrived, the men dressed
in trim white uniforms, and proceeded to put on a
concert for the people at the tables. There were four
kids playing in a dusty spot near me and it was fascinating to watch the way the music excited them. They
started jumping like crickets, sending up dust, and assuming the strange poses that seem to be universal
among kids—gestures of power and control and of waving magic wands. They bent their arms and made

pumping motions and put their chests out. They traced mathematical figures in the air with their hands. A boy put his forehead against a fig tree, while behind him a girl in a coral dress struck poses, putting the back of her hand over her forehead, bending one leg and stretching the other out straight, like a high-fashion model.

All this time an old woman in black sat with her gnarled hands on her lap watching them. Her wrinkled face was a soft record of worry and work and sadness. Sitting there under the long draping leaves of a eucalyptus tree, she watched the kids with a strange coldness, as if she had seen it all too often, had seen them grow and become vain and selfish and full of bluster, and leave you, and now she'd had enough, and wanted out.

As you sit there watching this kind of thing, a soft breeze making your cigarette glow, as you get an occasional whiff of the licorice smell of ouzo, and watch old Greeks in panama hats pass, jacket sleeves hanging loose over their arms, while the planet Jupiter shines above a palm tree, you get a far more vivid feeling of the mystery of life and of mankind than you get from looking at the 3,500-year-old ruins of Knossos a few miles to the south.

Most of my treasured memories of travel are recollections of sitting. I used to sit for hours at a big sidewalk café in Nice on balmy afternoons, amid fallen leaves and cash-register stubs, in a kind of cocoon of noise from motorcycles and buses, fumes of carbon monoxide making a mist between the plane trees. I'd watch the other table-sitters, and the pigeons moving amid the customers' feet, the crowds of people passing along the street, the drivers shouting *"Alors!"* and getting out to look at dents in their fenders.

Once a trim little lean brown root of a man with a waist no bigger around than a tea plate appeared, wearing bright-blue pants about the shape of Oxford bags of the 1930's, a black embroidered vest, a jaunty red scarf wrapped around his neck and hanging over one shoulder, and a wide-brimmed Spanish hat. He came up in front of the tables beneath a tree, set a little canvas stool down on the curb, put a tambourine in its case on the stool, took out an accordion, walked briskly to another tree and butted his cigarette, hitched on his accordion, walked in a very ritualistic way around the corner, out of sight, and came back playing a tune, doing a very stylish dancing kind of walk, looking over one shoulder in that fancy Spanish way, weaving between the people at the sidewalk tables, the noise level of the street nearly drowning him out. Then he put his accordion on his stool and did the whole choreography over again with castanets. Then he repeated it with the tambourine, shouted, *"Olé,"* came around with a tiny dish, collected something from almost everyone, put his castanets and tambourine inside the case—snap, snap—folded his stool—snap—and disappeared into the crowd on the sidewalk—self-contained, self-sufficient, mobile and free.

I also used to watch a middle-aged French woman who was more interesting than a medieval castle. There's something about a middle-aged French woman that's very different from a middle-aged English-speaking American or Canadian woman. The French woman looks more worldly and cynical. There's an absence of innocence about her as she sits there grimly religious, with her wicker basket of bread sticks, her peppers and tomatoes. You feel that she's centuries older than a woman at home in the A&P. You can't imagine her getting sentimental over Christmas or a wedding. You can imagine her being gratified by a wedding, but not sentimental about it. You can't imagine her being disillusioned about a husband. This woman had a mirthless face, still handsome, with a sulky lower lip and big round eyes. A gypsy kid—lean, straggly-haired, dirty-looking—came up and held out his hand to the woman, shoving a thin arm out, bent almost backward. The woman almost came out of her chair with emotion as she gave him a barrage of French, warning him off in an outraged voice, perhaps in shame for mankind. The kid disappeared into the crowd. The woman looked around indignantly, still smouldering.

11

Getting to Know the Real *Greeks*

One sad outcome of the age of universal travel is that the word "tourist" has acquired many of the connotations of, say, "smog," and everyone is trying desperately not to be mistaken for one. A while ago I watched a trimly dressed man in gold-rimmed glasses come down the arrivals ramp of an airport accompanied by a big load of luggage. He looked around at the crowd of common tourists with a little smile, as if rather amused that just hours ago he had been looking through those same gold-rimmed spectacles into the murderous eyes of a charging black rhinoceros. A gaunt young travel-game player crossed in front of him wearing scuffed canvas shoes and no socks and carrying nothing but a tennis racket and a red plastic bag with "Tokyo" on it, giving the impression that he had become so used to jetting around the world that now he just took along anything that he happened to be holding in his hand, and on my score card he won the point, game, set and match. But *he* was topped a shade, I thought, by a man with a beard who came through the doors carrying one small leather-bound book and a mountain climber's pick, neatly dropping both the tennis player and the big-game hunter into a crevasse. Following him came a man with a suit slung over his shoulder, travelling that way, one felt, because when he arrived in, Paris, perhaps, he just had time for a quick change before going out to an interesting dinner at the home of a friend, a movie producer, say.

By the time you've watched travellers for a while you begin to imagine that the pieces of luggage coming off the carousel are themselves acting out little bits of drama to distinguish them from the common tourist's luggage. I watched a big, rugged cowhide bag with a beer belly come off the belt looking as if it were smoking a cigar, muscle a plaid cloth bag aside, punch an attaché case, and get grabbed by a man in dark glasses. A pure white leather bag appeared on the roller, took an alarmed look around, swooned and fell to the bottom of the carousel with, it was easy to imagine, the back of its hand pressed against its forehead.

I left the bags to their own little games and wandered over and talked to a shoeshine man, who, without looking up from my feet, said women with children were spoiling the travel business. I discovered after a bit of probing, his objection was that they travelled just to *get* somewhere. I saw what he meant. While I was there a man giving off a faint scent of cologne hurriedly stepped up to the stand next to me, said in a clear voice that he just had time for a quick brushing up between Copenhagen and Mexico City, gave the shoeshine man a dollar and hurried off. His neat little play was watched cynically by a woman who was flaked out on a chair nearby in a kind of nest of hot-water bottles, coats, baskets, paper cups, blankets and babies. You could tell from her expression that she was about as impressed with paying someone a dollar for a shoeshine as she was with Hugh Hefner.

Travel snobbery is becoming more and more difficult, although young people still manage it with a neat reverse twist, travelling like old-time hobos, being haughty about any traveller who doesn't mingle with the people. One young guy who lived in a Volkswagen van parked behind my hotel in Heraklion was always telling me that he was getting to know the *real* Greeks, as if the Greeks I met were stuffed and imported.

As a matter of fact, nobody will ever get to know the Greeks in anything less than thirty years. I remember once watching a Greek woman guide on a tour that stopped at the site of an ancient palace (there's nothing wrong with guided tours if you regard them as a good way to get around, and don't worry about what the guide is saying and just watch her instead, for she can teach you most about Greece when she doesn't know she's doing it). A swarthy, fierce-looking Cretan with a dotted blue-black turban and cummerbund, knee-length boots, grey moustache, and gleaming black eyes, came up and began selling crude hand-made reed flutes from a tray that hung from his neck. The guide, a very soft-voiced Greek woman, tried to get a better one for me than the one I'd bought, and it turned into a peculiar, gentle cosy little affair, almost a secret process, like the Eleusinian mysteries. It couldn't have been learned, or understood, any other way than the way a kid in New York learns to play kick the can. The woman's hands were very close to the tray, so that her face and the man's were only inches apart. Both kept murmuring while their hands moved, with him handing her flutes, and her making gestures of putting them back at the bottom, while he took them

back very gently. It was a kind of continuous game of
three walnuts. She smiled and murmured and once
broke the reed off one, smiling and talking and sticking it back in the tray, and I expected him to pull a
saber and kill her on the spot, but he burst out laughing, displaying three or four gold teeth. I had the feeling that he would happily join in the game and break
a few more.

They looked as if it was all more fun than making
money, and they looked as if they could play the game
all day. For them the tourists had disappeared, the
bus had disappeared. The flutes disappeared. They
were just two humans who had been children at the
same time in the same land, and knew one another the
way they knew their own streets. You wouldn't have
been surprised if they'd linked arms and started to
dance and forgotten the whole tour, along with the
palace, although according to his price structure he
had just lost about 300 per cent of his net profit.

I had a similar experience when my wife and I were
on a cruise around the Aegean and Gulf of Corinth.
We were on a small (seventy-five-foot) launch. The
captain, a wiry, cheerful Greek with a dapper black
moustache, and his wife, who was the ship's cook,
were from the island of Mytilene, near the coast of
Asia Minor. We were tied up at Naupactus when a
wind called a *melteni*, which comes out of a clear blue
sky, and which used to confound the ancient Greek
navies, began whipping up the waves. It started things
swaying, heaving and creaking. The skipper had to decide whether to make a run for the Corinthian canal,
only a mile or so away, and his wife came out of the
galley and stood beside him. It was fascinating to
watch the two of them, no longer skipper and cook, but

a man and wife who knew those waters the way a man and wife in New York know traffic. They were a team, standing side by side at the prow, looking anxiously toward a thin line of foam on the horizon, taking turns looking through the glasses, saying things quietly to one another.

They decided to make the run. Their daughter came out and captured her cat and held it in her arms. A deck hand closed the portholes and stowed bags under bunks. There was a wonderful wild fifteen minutes of water lashing the windows, the horizon tilting and shimmering, the world rolling, then we were cruising serenely through the rocky slot of the Corinthian canal, everyone in a picnic mood, and the captain's wife back making supper. But I still remember them standing there looking at the sea that the Greeks had been sailing for three thousand years, and somehow it left me with a feeling that to really know these two Greeks you'd have to go back at least to the time of Ulysses.

Fijians Smile More

Rapid transportation has contributed to the noise that is thickening modern man's eardrums and causing ulcers and, some believe, heart attacks, but it also provides its own antidote—the means of escaping quickly to some quiet place like the Fiji Islands, where you can submerge for a while in the vanishing world of silence.

It's a strange experience to visit a place like the city of Nadi, on the north shore of the main island of Viti Levu. You can go for a stroll in the evening and hear sounds you've just about forgotten—the slap of a door in the evening, the crow of a rooster, the sound of an old man scolding a cow that won't go in the right direction, a kid calling to his grandfather. Walking along the street you become practically hypnotized by the peace and tranquility. Someone calls, "Hello, Mac. Haircut?" You hear the voice of an Australian visitor telling a friend that some bloody thing in a store window bloody well doesn't work. You hear a faint thumping sound coming from an open doorway, and see an Indian boy ironing a shirt. A storekeeper puts up some blue shutters. Someone calls drowsily, "Hey, chief, shine your shoes?"

One time when my wife and I were staying at the

Travelodge Motel in Suva, I was sitting by an open
window when I heard a soft, rustling sound I couldn't
place. It came from out of the night, floating across
Victoria Parade, one of the main boulevards. I finally
went out into the street to see what it was, crossed to
the grounds of the government buildings, and found
that what I had been hearing, and puzzling over, was
a sound I'd never heard before—the sound of a big
crowd of gentle people, something more strange and
remote from modern life than the Pyramids or the Temple of Athene. The people were promenading in the
soft evening light that filtered down through a kind of
trellis formed by the branches of big winding fig trees
and banyan trees that send roots down from their
branches like stalactites.

The feeling of the evening was utterly foreign and
exotic. There were individual sounds—a sandal scuff-
ing, a girl laughing, someone calling softly to a friend.
There were faces so beautiful that I stopped and stared
—an Indian girl with a smile like a jewel, her black face
framed in a lime-green scarf; a brown-faced Fijian
woman with an expression that came up from depths of
composed friendliness, tall, ample, barefooted and
high-breasted, with a halo of soft black hair as thick as
a brush.

Fiji has more than 800 islands, only 100 of them
inhabited, ranging from a patch of coral with a tuft
of coconut palms to the main island of Viti Levu, which
appears out of the Pacific like a mirage, 3,200 miles
southwest of Honolulu, its blue mountains draped in
clouds. As your plane starts to weave into its approach
pattern to Nadi Airport, you look down on a tapestry
of hedged farmlands, then coral reefs like stains of
rust and verdigris green in water so clear you don't

know you're looking through it. We made a hundred-mile shore hop on a stubby Fiji Airways DC-3 to Suva, and wandered around, feeling the peacefulness seep into our muscles in the mellow, yellow afternoon light, with the clouds rolling in off the Pacific and the same breeze that blew Captain Bligh between the islands bending the coconut palms. Downtown Suva is made up of rambling old wooden buildings, with sidewalk pillars wrapped in coconut fronds, and hotel balconies where you expect to see one of Somerset Maugham's planters waiting for sundown to have his first gin sling. There was a pleasant scene the day I was there—a nicely dressed Fijian housewife face down and sound asleep on the grass in a park, her shopping bag and her purse lying beside her.

The Fiji Islands were among the last South Pacific islands to be explored. Abel Tasman, the Dutch East India Company navigator, who in 1642 had found Tasmania and New Zealand (somehow he missed Australia), was the first to see them. He had been caught in a hurricane in a maze of coral reefs and afterward glimpsed a few headlands through the rain and mist. Nearly a century and a half later, Captain Cook touched on a tiny island at the far south of the group and saw a few natives disappearing into the bush. But the man who got the first really good look at the islands was the British navy captain William Bligh. When his men put him and eighteen officers overboard and set them adrift in an open boat, he passed between Viti Levu and Vanua Levu, managing to outrun a Fijian war canoe, and survived to come back and take a better look at the islands. The traders—British, American, Dutch, French, Australian—who in the early 1800's began to come to Fiji for sandalwood and an edible sea slug called bêche-de-mer, were the shoddiest group in Fijian history, since they demonstrated the miraculous power of guns by shooting naked spearmen.

One of the memorable things about Fiji for tourists who, if they're anything like I am, dislike happy faces on car bumpers, optimists' clubs, smiling politicians and all forms of aggressive good cheer and high spirits used like exploding cigars, is the natural cheerful friendliness in Fiji. The children, who speak in soft, husky voices as if trying not to wake up a sleeper about ten feet away, smile and wave at you as they knock mangoes from the trees on their way home from school, and they use brilliant red hibiscus flowers in the same sort of way kids in Canada or the United States stick maple seeds on their noses. A Fijian youngster standing beneath a rain tree waiting for a bus at the head of some lush, misty valley, or walking in a strong warm breeze past a sunny cane field, will put a hibiscus behind each ear, one in his hair and hold another in his mouth, and stand looking at the oncoming traffic, a strange little figure with a face made up of four red splotches.

The last day my wife and I were in Fiji an Indian cab driver drove us through some beautiful countryside, past some scenes that looked as if they were lovingly composed by an inspired set designer, like one I remember of some distant female figures in colored saris coming down a green mountain. At one place he asked an old Fijian working in a garden up on a hill to show us some tapioca plants, and the man disappeared over the hill. He came back with about twelve smiling Fijians of all ages—men, women and children—and one of the women had a plate of cooked tapioca root for us to taste.

Another time a Fijian and his wife and children were

in a coconut grove beside the road. The cab driver
spoke to him and told him we'd like to taste some milk
from a green coconut and the Fijian, with a touching
eager friendliness, picked one and speared the outer
husk on the tines of a pitchfork, which his son held
upright for him, leaned on the coconut and pried the
fibre loose. Then he trimmed the green coconut kernel
with a machete, lopped off the top and gave it to his
little girl to hand to me. She came up to me clearly
divided between nervousness and fascination at anyone
so unlike what, to her, fathers look like.

That evening I went for a walk and came to a bridge
over a valley that was vivid green right to the banks
of a muddy river. A girl of about twelve was sitting in
the river, in her dress, doing the family washing. I went
down and spoke to her. She gave me a smile about five
inches wide, every inch sincere, as if she could have sat
there smiling for ever just with the pleasure of my company. She rolled back lazily and disappeared, under-
water, then reappeared about fifteen feet upstream,
and rolled around like a seal. Sometimes just her feet
were visible sticking up out of the river, then just her
bottom, then her face, stomach and toes.

Three women came down to the river and walked
past her into the water, carrying loads of firewood.
They didn't hike their dresses or change their pace.
They just walked through the river to the other side,
came up on the green bank and disappeared slowly
down the valley toward some blue mountains that were
caught in swirls of clouds. Behind me a Fijian boy was
lazily trying to lasso a brown calf, which kept trying to
hide behind its mother. An old man led a cow past on
a rope, stopped, scolded the cow, flipped his jacket at
her and shooed her into a yard. A boy passed with a

cow and a heifer. A Brahman bull downstream looked at me languidly, as if he knew bulls were supposed to be ferocious, but he just couldn't be bothered on such a nice evening. The girl's head emerged from the river. She smiled and waved.

When I went back to my hotel I got talking to a Chinese restaurant operator who told me he was largely responsible for having some posters taken down which had said, "Keep Smiling." He told me that he had said to the people who put them up, "What the hell are you talking about? They've *always* been smiling." I asked him who had thought up the poster and he said, "Some smart guy." The posters urging people to smile had already started people getting mad, and this among people who probably smile more, from the bottom of their hearts, than any people on earth.

I Like Cars,
Niagara Falls and Florida

With world travel as commonplace as bingo, the traveller faces a tough job finding some place that at least *feels* as if he discovered it himself. One way to solve the problem is simply to accept it, take a reverse course, and go some place everybody has discovered—like North America, preferably in your car. If you mention that you like car trips, some world traveller just back from Nepal is apt to look at you as if you went out with inner tubes and side curtains and ask with kindly amusement what you *do* on motor trips; and you know when you mention it that a lot of people are wondering how you can stand that gaudy highway culture and those highway signs—2.5 MILES TO THE THING!—and the souvenir shops with funny gifts to send back home, like miniature toilets. What I do is steer past them.

I love motor trips. I began making them in a ten-year-old Chevrolet with our luggage lashed to the running board with rope, and I haven't missed making at least one trip a year ever since. I like the feeling of being detached from my fellow man, and those lonely roadside conversations with gas-station operators who appear out of dimly lit caves of fan belts and batteries

and, while they're wiping my windshield, impart little
bits of information ("That dog there? That's a genuine Australian coconut hound. The only one north of
the equator.") and then disappear, leaving me standing
alone in the night wind with the tumbleweed blowing
against my pants, not quite sure where I am except
that it's somewhere on Route 66.

I like lying in bed in motels listening to the trucks
shift gears on a distant grade, and occasionally spending
twenty-five or thirty dollars for a motel and wallow-
ing voluptuously in decadent luxury and crass materi-
alism and romping mother-naked over an acre of broad-
loom and King-size beds with Magic fingers in the
breeze of the air conditioner. I never feel more alive
than when I check out of a rumpled motel room in the
morning with a feeling that I'm leaving an old camp-
site, and head down the highway with the morning
sun coming straight down on my knees.

You don't need a guide to tell you what to look at
when you see a coyote loping across the highway in
the pink light of dawn, or when the hard-rock forest
of the Canadian Shield opens up west of Kenora into
the Canadian prairies, like the opening bars of a sym-
phony, or when the Rockies appear, no higher than
anthills, on the horizon to the west of Calgary. I've
never crossed the desert without pulling off onto a road
like the one between Blythe and Needles, wandering
up an arroyo and building a fire just to hear the twigs
sizzle and to feel the hot sun on my back and listen to
the silence, which is something few of us ever hear.
One time I was puzzled by a strange ticking noise until
I discovered that what I was hearing was the sound of
my wristwatch. Another time it started to rain, just a
few drops hitting the rocks, but it was as dramatic an

event as I've ever heard. The very bushes looked tense and expectant. It must have been a bit like that when the first rains began to cool the rocks in the beginning of the world.

You don't need to know a Giotto from a get-well card to appreciate the sight of a group of working cowboys, as you hear their whistles float toward you from the distance, light as thistledown on the clear desert air, or to enjoy the smell of timber in Northern Ontario or the old, wild, wet wind of Niagara Falls.

People who live around the Great Lakes, a region bigger than France, are very self-conscious about enjoying the Falls. "You're at Niagara *Falls?*" a young woman editor said to me recently at the other end of a long-distance call: "*No*body goes to Niagara Falls." She gave a hoot of mirth as I looked out at a crowd of about 27,000 sightseers (the day's quota of the 15 million who visit Niagara Falls annually), which at that moment included five amateur photographers shouting things like "Just walk slowly toward me!" and a father who called out, as his wife lurched with alarm toward her son, "Let him fall over if he wants to!" evidently up to here with eight-year-old boys who want to get a closer look at the rapids, and a man from Australia, who had come 10,000 miles to see, among other things, Niagara Falls. "I've read about it in *National Geographic,* of course," he said, with a tone of faint disbelief, watching the overflow from the world's biggest lakes drop into a rock canyon with a magnificent earth-shaking roar.

One of the great travel buys in the world is the cruise on the *Maid-of-the-Mist,* the little steamer that goes right up to the base of the Horseshoe Falls. The last time I was there, the round trip was $1.50, plus twenty cents for the descent by inclined railway to the river's edge at the bottom of the gorge. You're given a heavy black oilskin with a medieval cowl, and as you stand there under a bright blue sky it all seems overly cautious, to the point of being theatrical.

The passengers crowd up to the bow, making jokes, their voices muffled by the hoods. They look like a little knot of departing souls waiting to be ferried into the underworld. As the boat moves out from the dock, the river seems much like any other river, except that there's tremendous suction pulling the stern around and causing a slight list until the bow is headed into the current. You cruise upriver, past a rainbow at the base of the American Falls, where, due to several cave-ins, rocks have piled up to perhaps a third the height to the brink, and on toward the Horseshoe Falls. There's a roar in the air that grows steadily more powerful. You begin to feel a bit of a breeze.

There's something very ominous up ahead. You can hear it and sense it. The black hooded figures strain to see it. The day seems to be getting darker. The river becomes choppy and now you're passing between whirlpools. You have the feeling somehow that you're entering a place where you have no right to be. There's a dense mist ahead. The wind whips the passengers' hoods and the roar makes it hard for them to hear each other. The boat trembles and shudders and rocks. The mist is now being driven before a high wind, drenching the oilskins that you're now grateful to be wearing.

You realize that the falls are now far up over your head, curling over the lip, a faint yellowish grey dark moving mass. You're right inside a weird world.

There's a Creature there, all around you, strange and terrifying.

You think it couldn't get any wilder. Then the boat turns her bow straight into the falls. There's a great rumble and vibration of her engines and she begins bucking three-foot waves that roar out at her like a defending army, out of the mist. They fight the *Maid-of-the-Mist* to a standstill; then, with an air as if she has tested her strength with this enemy every day for years, and has always failed, the boat gives up once more, sweeps around, carried by the onslaught of the current, and drifts back to the normal world down-river.

A strange thing happened the last time I took a trip on the *Maid-of-the-Mist*. There was a couple on board: a girl in a leather jacket and high boots and a hefty young man with a couple of professional-looking cameras— Both were pretty patronizing and it was evident that they wanted to let everyone know that they'd seen exotic sights in remote lands and weren't the common run of yokel who is impressed by Niagara Falls. But they both got quieter as the boat nosed into the maelstrom around the Horseshoe Falls, and finally, when we were right in the thick of it, the girl, startled out of every last shred of pose, just looked around in awe, and shouted to her companion, above the roar. "Oh, Frank—it's beautiful!" She looked rather beautiful herself at that moment, which may be one of the effects of getting that close to something so awesome. Everyone who can, should take a cruise on the *Maid-of-the-Mist* at least once a year.

Another North American tourist attraction that has a peculiar reputation is Florida. It has become so symbolic of everything that's brash and vulgar that some people take a certain pride in never having been there. In the case of Florida, there is some justification for this. It's full of the kind of promoter whose idea of the wonders of nature is to pave it, build a shopping plaza over it, or convert it into Disney World or condominiums, and who loves to put pants on chimpanzees, teach elephants to water-ski, train porpoises in funny hats to make hideous noises as if blowing little tin bugles and to teach girls to smile ten feet under water in glass tanks, as if they really don't need to breathe.

But there's a real Florida, with real kids who lasso little lizards with long blades of grass and proudly walk along with them on threadlike leashes on the way home from school, and real dunes, enclosing a hot, thorny, twiggy world of cactus and Spanish bayonet where little bright green lizards blow up vermillion balloons from their throats and where at the sight of a human, tortoises pull in their heads with a sound of escaping air, like a leak in an air mattress, and everything is hot and still the way the world must have been before living things came up out of the sea.

One of the great travel experiences is to spend Christmas in Florida. It breaks up a lot of old patterns of thought, better than Scrooge's tour with Marley's ghost, and the northern visitor finds that all those years that he has been saying, with a whimsical little shake of his head, "Christmas wouldn't be Christmas without snow," he has been wrong.

There's nothing un-Christmaslike about what native Floridians call a "pretty" day. The salt spray glistens in the air like crystals, the palms sparkle in the morning sun, and the big translucent leaves of banana trees shine like illuminated Christmas displays. Real porpoises without hats rocket around inside waves as bright as a promise, mockingbirds sing on the needle-sharp leaves of century plants, and billions of white butterflies float between the dunes.

While up North the hysteria of mass merchandising lies over the land like a nerve gas, and grown men try to hide hangovers and exclaim, "Just what I wanted!" over new snowmobiles and power mowers, down in Florida you sit with your feet up in an old frayed deck chair as happy as old Bob Cratchit, looking out at a lazy sea that makes a muffled crackling sound, like a giant walking over distant orange crates, watching pelicans coasting through waves that look as if they'd been drawn across the sea with a felt pencil. You feel like exclaiming, "A splendid bird!" "A most admirable ocean!" and "A Merry Christmas, one and all!"

With no distraught shoppers or desperate drinkers or downtown traffic tied up with slush to cope with, people are free to think of the religious significance of Christmas. My wife and I started going to New Smyrna Beach, an East Coast Town, when our daughters were small. We'd leave our home town in the North, with friends feeling sorry for the children being dragged around like that—and at such a Christian time of year! —and we'd no sooner arrive than our daughters would be involved in something at the school or church. School kids painted biblical scenes and set them in illuminated wooden frames on top of cypress posts around the public library lawn. We'd drive over into the town from the beachside at night when all was silent and still, and there was a faint smell of the sea in the air, and the moon lit the old clapboard houses and threw a holy light on the cabbage palms. Sometimes we'd watch a Christmas pageant, sitting on bleachers beside an old park lit by the Florida moon. Or maybe something would be taking place in the Sunday school and you'd enter some bright and buzzing church basement and sit on hard benches and listen to someone with a soft South Carolina accent read the Gospel of St. Luke, her face lit by candlelight, and watch a tableau in which you personally knew the Virgin Mary, who usually caught the school bus outside your house, and you'd recognize Joseph beneath his bath-towel robes as a gangling kid you'd wanted to belt the night before for cleaning you out of Cokes. You really got the feeling of peace on earth and good will toward men.

A few days before Christmas we'd drive out to some Florida backwoods to gather pine boughs and pine cones, and pick holly and mistletoe. There are enough deciduous trees in Florida to make a carpet of dead leaves in the woods, and sometimes you hear the scampering sound of an escaping armadillo, which, in spite of its tortoiselike appearance, can run like a rabbit. My wife made a crèche of twigs from a bay tree, thatched it with palmetto fronds and shredded more fronds to make hay for the manger. We still have it in the locker of our northern apartment, and I can't look at it without my thoughts drifting off to Christmases Past in Florida.

Sometimes we'd get a cold snap, and the ocean became black and white instead of pale green, and the foam lay shivering on the beach like Jell-O and the gulls all faced the northeast, squinting into the wind. We'd hear over the radio that it was going down to thirty in central Florida and to twenty-nine in the mucklands. (I never did find out what the mucklands were, but they sounded wonderfully remote and primitive.) There'd be a hum of oil trucks around the beach, and living room heaters would be turned on. In the older houses, live-oak logs would be carried in to the fireplaces. Neighbors called, wearing sweaters, and asked cheerfully, "Did you hear the news? It's going down to freezing tonight!" After supper, you'd open the door and the moon looked as hard and cold as a new half dollar, and the roar of the ocean seemed louder. Neighbors would go out to pick the poinsettias before they froze, calling to one another like northerners shovelling snow. It couldn't have been more like Christmas if Santa Claus had come out from behind a yucca bush.

But just as often, or more often, the weather was hot and summery, and sometimes windy, with crows doing airborne dances on top of the slash pines and the mullet running and the pelicans dropping like stones into the sea and the palms showing bald spots as they bowed their heads in the wind, and there'd be a great feeling of excitement in nature. But there was no lessening of the feeling of Christmas and holidays. Kids were out of school. Grandmothers brought their small grandchildren down to the beach with their new sand pails and shovels and the kids sat down abruptly without bending their legs and started to dig right through to China to see if everyone was really hanging upside down there. Every now and then a baby who had just discovered the marvels of walking would take off down the beach. The tiny figure silhouetted against the ocean and moving behind a fringe of sea oats would be heading for distant lands until he was scooped up in mid flight by a loving parent, which must be a frustrating experience.

Youths surfed, or tried to, an inspiring lesson in making the best of what you've got, in this case the wrong ocean; although Atlantic waves have the power to shift sea walls and are mean infighters, they're stubby and break too soon for surfing. But high-school kids with torsos like wieners, wearing frayed and dripping shorts, would be out there at dawn, when the rising sun made a yellow mist of the salt crystals and the sea had a soft and sudsy sound and looked like boiling gold. At first you wouldn't know anyone was out there. Then you'd notice a human head out in the foam, like a floating coconut, or see a surfboard shoot up out of the foam.

Most surfers rarely go more than a few feet. They fall as soon as they stand up, then lie belly-down on the board and hand-paddle out to sea again, and go on learning concentration, balance, hope, faith and how to take pratfalls, while, inland, promoters advertise frantically that the secret of life is being eternally happy doing nothing in some awful development with a name like Whispering Palms Mobile Homes. The surfers don't look happy. They look half drowned, and as they walk slowly back for supper carrying their surf-boards, they stare at their toes and look worried, trying to figure out what they did wrong, and can do right next day. But they know that life is a struggle, and happiness has nothing to do with it, and the girls, who rarely surf but lie around in sun-tan lotion giving the off-ocean breeze the fragrance of Cleopatra's barge, look out to sea toward the surfers, knowing that that's where the future is, and that the past is sitting up on the porch of a Whispering Palms Mobile Home in a shuffleboard hat—or is a thousand miles north, sitting knee-deep in torn Christmas wrappings saying Christmas wouldn't be Christmas without snow.

Not in My *Holy Land*

Now that everyone can actually *see* the places of legend and literature—the shrine at Delphi (where guides point out with a straight face the three holes made by the oracle's tripod); the castle of Elsinore that was haunted by the ghost of Hamlet's father; the site where Caesar was assassinated, or, anyway, where the guide *says* he was assassinated—"right there"—mankind will soon have nothing left to his imagination. "I've *seen* it," is a clincher that stops the free flow of conversation. Fundamentalists make this kind of thing work for them. "They've actually found a place where there was a flood," they say triumphantly. "I saw the high-water mark when Mabel and I were in the Holy Land."

Not in *my* holy land they didn't. Floods that leave high-water marks happen in places like Shreveport, Louisiana; *The* Flood took place in a place of imagination, literature, philosophy, morals, parable and thought, and should stay there, along with places like Christ's sepulchre, now a tourist attraction in the old city of Jerusalem, reinforced with steel and, when I was there, under repairs, like a bank. It's a good illustration of why these things shouldn't be dealt with like real estate, pinned down, owned, labelled, walled, surveyed and registered. The tourist learns more looking for Christian acts in live people. They're harder to find, but a lot more rewarding.

To get to the Holy Sepulchre, you go through a frightening warren jam-packed with humanity, and your pilgrimage gets less and less spiritual the further you go. You don't know whether you're between old walls or right inside one wall. There's a confusion of overhead arches, passageways, doorways, roofs, windows, overhanging eaves. It's dank, murky, and smelly, with side stalls hollowed out of the stones and stuffed with pigs, nail polish, eggs, stoves, grapes, chocolate bars, beans, rugs, dresses, hassocks. Tunnels open off tunnels. It has the feeling of a subterranean world, as if you're being shoved through an old endless culvert with shops cut into the wall. Men call, "Hallo, just come and look," as you go down and down further into the labyrinth, shoved along shoulder to shoulder with Arabs, beggars, priests, babies, widows.

You wonder nervously if it will ever end. You can't see the sky any more, but the crowd shoves you on. Sometimes someone holds a finger against the small of your back, shoving, and eventually appearing in front of you, and you find yourself wondering if this is the original meaning of "The first shall be last and the last shall be first." In this packed corridor, incredibly, an unattended donkey shoves past you, walking between you and a counter of eels. There's manure on the pavement, something I don't really mind, but some of the smells from the stalls make you whip around as if someone shouted at you, or was creeping up on you. It's hot. A calico cat crosses the cobbles with a piece of chicken gut dangling from its mouth. Some of the doorways in the rocks are just dark holes, concealing bandits for all you know. An endless mob can be seen ahead of you, going, like a human river, down as far as you can see, past dimly lit caves, past pots and pans and dead chickens, hides and jewelery, pigeons, caged birds, piles of fish, meat, bread. Two men hammer at some kind of sheet metal object; a blowtorch bursts into flame at your elbow. You wonder if you should forget Christ's tomb and try to get out and up to the open sky. You look up some side streets, but they disappear into a brown murk and look even more forbidding than the one you're following, swept along by the human current.

Finally you come to the Church of the Holy Sepulchre. You go inside, through another doorway, and into a low-ceilinged chamber about the size of one parking space, which is dimly lit by candles, and smells of melting wax. You move dubiously toward another opening about four feet high, from which emerges the dim flickering of candles, and the sound of sobbing. You bend down and look through the passageway, but can make out only the lower half of two women in black. An attendant comes up and calls gruffly to them to clear out and make way for the paying visitors. An old woman backs out like an old turtle, still sobbing. Two more old women come out. The attendant beckons to you. You bend over and go in. A black-robed priest explains that right under that marble slab Christ was buried and you can touch it if you like, and that there at the side is the very rock Christ moved from his tomb and if you'd like to leave some money to help with reconstruction of the church, you can. He indicates a tray loaded with folding money, just like the tray in front of a hat-check girl.

You leave and wander around in a bit of a daze. Another man calls to you—pssst!—Come in this side. On the other side, the one you just came out of, you don't really see the rock Christ moved. It's covered with marble or something. Here. "Kneel right down here and take a look." That's the real rock. You kneel and peer up under this little grotto with the smell of burning wax in your nose and your face about a foot from a black, greasy-looking ledge of rock, and another tray full of folding money and you drop some more money in it and leave, wishing you could call back your original vague visions of biblical scenes that you remember from your old Sunday-school papers.

The fact is, if travel is going to mean anything, the modern traveller to the Holy Land (or to any other land) will have to take a less literal outlook than his predecessors, including the first travellers of ancient times, when the great travel objective was to see the seven wonders of the world—the pyramids, the lighthouse at Alexandria, the hanging gardens of Babylon, the Temple of Diana in central Italy, the tomb of King Mausolus in Asia Minor, the Colossus of Rhodes, and the statue of Zeus at Olympia. These things were remote and exotic, and the very physical act of seeing them was an adventure. Now you can see them all— or their counterparts—on color TV while you're having supper.

But with a shift in attitude, the very technology and ease of travel that have made viewing the world's unusual sights a commonplace (and often a disillusioning experience) are the same means that can give a visit a more subtle, and a more basic meaning. The visiting Ford dealer from Hamilton, Ontario, who expects something special to happen when he visits the Holy Land, wants to be convinced by miracles. But Christianity, which began here, and swept the Roman Empire, was not a building. And it wasn't a holy site. It was (and, ideally, still is) a new outlook, so novel and opposed to good practical common sense, that few people really believe in it, or have tried it, although many have talked about it. The character and cast and problems of the Bible are still here for the tourist to observe, like man's apparent determination to wipe himself out. The Wailing Wall is secured by barbed wire, and at the entrance to the area, an Israeli soldier sits with a gun across his knees, waving you toward a handsome, blue-eyed, brown-faced Israeli girl who sits with a gun across *her* knees and who searches the women's handbags to make sure that no member of some other great religion has put a bomb in the purse.

You meet churchly characters, proud of their virtues and how scrupulously they observe the rules laid down by God. While I stood looking at the Wailing Wall, where some people stood with their foreheads pressed into the rocks and others rocked and chanted, in an utterly unpeaceful big barren area from which emitted a bedlam of sound—chants, wails, shouts and sobs—a fierce-looking man in a blue suit and black hat and dark-rimmed glasses who had been pacing up and down reading aloud, stopped, glared at me, and made furious gestures indicating that I was to go over to a card table piled with paper hats and put one on my head. When I came back, holding it to my head with one finger like a Victorian lady in a strong breeze, he gave me a stern look of triumph, the same look that comes into the eyes of all dedicated people who have sharply drawn attention to the thing they are dedicated to, like people with patriotic bumper stickers. A Jewish woman with fine, floating hair, who stood on the feminine side of the Wailing Wall, looked across at me with an expression that made me think she was no more impressed by all this strict dedication to ritual than, say, a wife attending women's night at a Kiwanis dinner. She grinned at me and gave a good-natured shrug, as if she were telling me that they were out of pickled herrings.

You get the feeling that things around the Wailing Wall are about the same as things around Chicago or Belfast, on the brink, and that the Holy Land isn't getting any holier. But there are more lessons in store for the tourist once he stops looking at old holy sites and starts looking at people, and even observing his own mixed and confused thoughts as he gets jostled around on these turbulent cultural waters on which the visitor from North America floats along, a rather odd-looking chip.

For instance, Arab kids follow you, offering to show you where Christ's tomb is. You wonder uneasily whether it's because you look rich or stupid or both, and you try to get rid of them mentally by telling yourself it's all an amusing, typical part of the travel scene, and perhaps you manage a cool little worldly smile. But they don't disappear. They're still there, trotting along at your side thoughtfully, real people, individual, lively, intelligent, with big dark eyes that look right through you. You next try being bluff and jovial, but they look a bit shocked and hurt and say disturbing things, like "You think I'm funny, do you?"— making you feel rotten. Then you're not quite sure whether or not beneath that earnest manner, they're laughing at you. One kid asked me for a cigarette, and when I said he looked too young to smoke, he said,

"It's not for me, it's for my fat uncle from Chicago, the windy city," without cracking a smile, right at a time when I was trying to lose thirty pounds.

You keep shifting your ground, trying to get your toes into some nice warm comfortable cliché that will make them disappear, but nothing works. You stop to look at some nail polish or can openers or other exotic wares for sale in the Holy City, hoping it will all blow over. The kids stand beside you looking at the merchandise with you, silent, plotting new tactics. Suddenly you want to belt them, a terrible commentary on 2,000 years of Christian love and kindness.

Somehow it comes to an end. "You go there and turn left," one of the kids says, fatalistically, looking at you sadly and pointing to the space between the knees of two people sitting facing each other outside a couple of stalls. The opening is about half the distance that separates people sitting facing each other on a bus—a kind of mud-colored tunnel between some rugs. You see through the trick immediately, but you don't blame the kids for giving you the wrong directions. You ask directions from a young man in one of the shops. He points the same way. "You go in there and at the next street turn left," just the way you were directed by the kids. You look back. The boys have faded back into the crowd, but their faces are still turned toward you. "You thought I was lying, didn't you?" the kid who gave you directions calls, looking hurt. You realize that he was being a good loser, and your conscience bothers you so much that the next kid you see you grab a handful of change and give it to him. He gives you one startled look and bolts, off to buy six popsicles, you hope.

A couple of incidents happened to me that, in themselves, made visiting the Holy Land worthwhile, and did more to remind me of Christian ideals than the tour of sacred sites. One was the way my wife and I were helped to find a room in Jerusalem, which was sold out by the girl in the information booth at Tel Aviv Airport. She was like a star, steady, serene and full of hope. She worried about us, without pose or pontification, her smallish, pale, earnest face full of concern, without turning on my airline stewardess charm, just working hard, trying to get us accommodation and transportation. Trying to save us money on cab fare, she faced eight cab drivers, all enjoying the sabbath while she worked, sitting around looking unspiritual, and she didn't get sore when they turned her down. When she was baffled, she didn't make excuses or lie, or try to save face by trying to put the blame on us for not making proper arrangements.

Once she walked about a quarter of a mile along the airport on a blistering hot day and just stood there in the hot sun looking back at us, worrying about us. When she came back, another harassed tourist got in front of us asking about accommodations and she told him, with great respect for *him,* that she would be with him as soon as she had looked after us, and I thought of all the clerks I'd had snarl at me, *"I'm busy!"* under the same circumstances. She was an infinitely patient girl, friendly to the human race, who never raised her voice above a gentle conversational Jewish tone and finally managed to get us a ride, and a room in a beautiful old hotel with rose-colored stone floors and a shady, breezy garden, with a palm tree, lime tree, oleander, cedars, climbing geraniums and bougainvillea.

The other incident was when we arrived back in Tel

Aviv, which, to anyone coming into it by bus from Jerusalem, is like an American desert town at its worst. We asked directions from a plump, perspiring man with a limp, who was wearing one of those little Jewish beanies and an expression of harassed friendliness. He went about eight blocks out of his way to show us where we wanted to go, lying rather badly that he always walked that far in the hot sun rather than take the bus, getting mixed up in his directions but staying in there, perspiring, until he knew that we were at the right place. I still see his anxious face, and that of the information girl, when I think of the Holy Land.

15

A Bullfight Without Blood

One of the most depressing results of expanding tourism is the rapid growth of fashionable resort areas that has taken place, red-tile roof by red-tile roof, every place where there's a beach, from Carmel to Malaga. They all look the same—quaint boats, cobbles, quaint stores, green glass floats, fishing nets, people buying things in quaint shops, photographers lining up to take the same pictures, and swingers behind stone walls drinking and being sophisticated.

One way to avoid all this triteness is to mark these places carefully on a map, then draw a straight line inland away from them and see where it brings you. If you do this from Cascais or Estoril in Portugal, you come out at a village called Santarem and (if you're as lucky as we were) find yourself at a big local fair, mingling with cows, bullocks, dust, horses, wagons, smells, cooking fish and people, and you can wander around eating probably the most delicious roast peanuts in the world. If you feel like it you can go to a Portuguese bullfight, the only tourist in the crowd. In a Portuguese bullfight they don't kill the bull, and if somebody *has* to torment an animal for amusement, and this seems to be a mania of man, from Calgary to

Madrid, and probably past that, you at least have the satisfaction of seeing the bull rack up a few tormentors and trot off without having to pay for it, although unfortunately he gets the wrong people. The ones you want to see him get are the posturing dandies on horseback who drive those barbs into his shoulder to the accompanying thump of a drum from the band, then raise their hats and prance around waving to the audience. But while you sit there getting whiffs of men's cologne and burning fish, and cheering for the bull as he tries to lob them over the bleachers, you grudgingly admire some guy with wavy hair who lets his horse dance sideways to the bull, always managing to escape the bull's charge. He rides past letting the bull get his horns within about a half an inch of the horse, holding his hat in the air, smiling at the audience as if he had no idea a bull was a fraction of an inch away, trying to kill him, an incredible combination of vanity, cruelty and magnificent horsemanship.

But the real highlight is the final act of these affairs. For sheer courage I've never seen the like of it. Portuguese bullfights have a peculiar ending. Eight men in green tights get out there in the ring and arrange themselves in a pattern resembling a sword, with the long end pointing at the bull. They have no swords or capes and no more protection than if they were standing out there in their pyjamas, and you have to remember that they're facing a full-size massive-chested fighting bull that, although his horns are padded, has tremendous crushing power and such a single-minded desire to kill something on two legs that during the earlier part of the fight, when one of the guys on foot with a cape runs for an opening in the arena wall, the bull will hit the fence with its feet in

the air and try to get right over the top of it, with a
great clattering and terrifying thump, scattering the
people on the inside of the partition. Although they are
safe, they can no more stand there that close to so
much fury than a man can keep his hand against the
outside of a glass case with a rattlesnake striking the
inside.

Now these men in the green tights and toques like
French-Canadian habitant caps, looking very small,
walk out and stand facing the bull with nothing between them and the bull but sand and sunlight. One
man stands far out in front with his hands on his hips
as the bull looks at him across the ring for a chilling
moment, clearly unable to believe his luck. Then he
drops his great battering ram of a head and comes at
the man like a guided missile. You can hardly believe
your eyes, but the guy stands there, does a little backward dance and takes the bull's head right on his
stomach. He grabs hold of the bull's horns, and while
he's being whipped up and down like a sack of wheat,
the other men pile onto the bull's head, hoping to hold
it still, but getting tossed and scattered. The day I
was there, the bull drove the leader into the ground,
and rolled him around until a man came out with a
cape and distracted the bull long enough for the other
men to carry the leader off, his face white and set in
pain. Then the men regrouped, with another man out
in front, replacing the one the bull had just disposed
of. The bull was obviously getting the feel of the thing,
and was doing an even better job of ramming the
second leader around than he had on the first when
again he was drawn off by a waving cape and the man
was carried off.

The thing I remember most about the afternoon was

the third man waggling his shoulders at the bull, inviting it to charge. It was the most impressive display of nonchalance in a rotten predicament I expect I'll ever see. I had already decided that this little guy had the worst job in the world, replacing the other two men who had been carried off by his mates. Now, instead of just running and catching the next train for some other country, he actually made taunting gestures at the bull, which stood on the opposite side of the ring with an expression of disbelief. The man gave his cap a little pat, shoved his hips forward one at a time as he strutted closer to the bull, clapped his hands, and gave this taunting waggle of his shoulders. Then the bull was coming at him, all out, and wham! the man was between the horns, going up and down just the way the other victims had, holding on, going down, getting rammed into the dirt, but this time holding on until the other men simply wrestled the bull to a standstill and held him. Then, as part of the ritual, they all suddenly scatter, except for one man who holds the bull by the tail. As the outraged bull pivots to get his horns under him and send him into orbit, the guy turns his feet out and skids around in a circle, still holding the tail; he keeps this up until about eight big brown oxen, apparently this bull's pals, are brought out into the ring, each jangling a cowbell, and the bull crowds in among them, puts his muzzle between their backs, and they all trot off the field together.

16

Before Other Tourists Are Awake

You don't really see anything when you barrel through the countryside on a tour bus, with some vacationing air-conditioner salesman sitting beside you calling out questions to the tour-guide, like how much windmills cost, and the driver leaning on his horn, scattering peasants like quail, and crossing himself on some sharp turn while the guide shouts that down in that valley on your right someone slew his father and married his mother. Often the guide points out what a fine driver we have today, and he would appreciate any little thing you feel like giving him at the end of the tour, when you're thinking he should be given a suspended sentence and more driving lessons.

You might see a lot of country, but you don't really feel its moods. The way to do that is to go for a walk, alone, preferably early in the morning before other tourists are awake. You can see things at your own pace, stop whenever you feel like it, stand and watch something simple, like a cow, or a fly buzzing near an old stone wall festooned with flowers, or a fisherman sailing out on an estuary as if giving you a private performance of how a sailboat should be handled as you stand there at the water's edge with wrinkled

waves coming in fast and hissing, and the wind rustling
the poplars and making ropes twang and, if you leave
your mouth open a bit, ballooning out your leeward
cheek.

Early morning is the time to visit cathedrals, too.
Going into these ancient buildings later in the day
with a guided tour is about as spiritual an experience
as going to an automobile show, but when you sit
there early in the morning, the only person in the place
except perhaps for an old woman kneeling up at the
altar, when you look at the colors the morning light
throws on the old stone floors and listen to the far-off
plonking sounds an empty cathedral makes, you get the
feeling that it's waiting for something.

Early-opening and all-night bars are administering
aid quietly but briskly to people with hangovers, who
sit staring into space, getting ready to face the day's
little defeats with good cheer. Watching the way people of various nationalities wake up is one of the great
travel experiences. I remember watching a Japanese
mathematics teacher on Tokyo TV extracting roots of
quadratic equations at five-thirty in the morning. When
he had the blackboard covered he'd suck in his breath
through his teeth, like someone taking a shower when
someone upstairs turned on the hot water and the
water below suddenly turned ice cold. Watching the
French wake up is even better than solving equations. A housewife with a string shopping bag comes
in, tosses off a brandy in two belts and goes on her
innocent way to face the day's chores. A woman with
big sad eyes sits looking at past mistakes sipping beer.

I can still see one man who came into a bar just
after sun-up, a short man in a peaked cap who somehow gave the impression that he had his suit on over

his pyjamas. After he had ordered his drink, he stood sideways to the bar as if he didn't know a drink had been set there by a kindly bartender, where it was winking at him in the morning sun. You could tell he just wanted to think about it for a while. Then he turned quickly and grabbed it as if catching it unawares, took his first sip, walked briskly to the front of the bar and looked out onto the street. Then he came back, lit a cigarette, hitched his shoulders, twiddled his fingers, turned a half-circle in one direction and then a half-circle in the opposite direction. You could see him coming to life, unfolding, like a morning glory. In the early morning you see what Parisians do that, by the time the tours start, around noon, has them all riding bicycles, carrying bread and kissing one another.

One advantage that walking has over tours is that you experience the moods of a city or town instead of just looking at its tourist attractions. On a tour of Tokyo, for instance, you go up onto a sight-seeing tower that looks just like the Eiffel Tower and visit a tea garden where you sit self-consciously with fifty other tourists watching a tea ceremony, put on for the tourists. But the real adventure is walking around a city of eleven and a half million, doing all the things you used to like to do in a strange big city, without worrying about getting mugged: moseying up some cosy, sunny slot of a street that runs beside and partly under an elevated railway; turning up an alley off an alley like a released tomcat; getting a shoeshine just to stand on a corner looking at some high buildings a mile away in a mist; wandering around in the late afternoon, when the sun is low in the south and the whole city is like a great golden beehive; or just watching the people.

You realize they don't even look Japanese. You see,

or think you see, everyone you've ever known, or worked with. Those pointless jokes about Japanese bowing and saying, "Ah so," seem even more pointless. Bowing is a friendly, courteous gesture that you'd like to see adopted back home, by bus drivers, for instance, or hockey players. A woman on the telephone saying, "A-a-a-a-!" pronouncing it in an amazed, high-pitched thin musical tone, doesn't sound funny—she sounds gentle, polite and civilized. (She also keeps saying "Hi" in a quick tight tone, an expression used like "right" or "okay," but which to a North American listener sounds as if the person on the other end of the phone is starting to hang up.)

On walks you make your own discoveries; for instance that Japanese school boys, in yellow caps, come home from school just like school boys in Larder Lake or Cleveland; in small circles, going around every lamp-post and parking meter. Small girls, passing in troops, dressed in tan uniforms, all talking at once, sound like geese. Each one as she passes you, waves tentatively, immediately crowding up against the kid ahead for safety, pretending she didn't do it. Teen-age girls working, for instance, in a McDonald's Hamburger, are like teen-age girls anywhere, good-natured, cheerful, a delight to deal with, thinking everything is fun—dropping a hamburger, not dropping a hamburger, taking a crack at saying "thank you" in English, or what's even more fun, listening to you try to say "thank you" in Japanese.

It's the things you see walking around by yourself at night, or in the early morning, that you remember most—a girl working at night in a brightly lit flower shop on a floor of wet trampled leaves; a woman sweeping cobbles under some ginko trees at dawn; a miniature landscape inside a dark doorway, made of rocks and real plants, with a castle about two inches high on top. You get the feeling discovering these things by yourself that you've taken them by surprise and that they were never expected to be seen or photographed or imitated by interior decorators, but were just developed for pleasure over centuries by real people like housewives, on frosty mornings, when the air was scented with woodsmoke.

One thing I still see when I think of Japan is a store no bigger than a kiosk where I stopped one night for some cigarettes. A plump youngster, helping her father, came out and I winked at her and suddenly realized that I was looking at the top of her round head and that she was making a deep bow, a nice little formality there on a dark street in the lamplight amid the peanuts and Texas bars, with her father looking pleased that she remembered her manners.

The next best thing to walking is taking tram rides, provided they're real old-time streetcars, which you find in Kyoto, Japan, and in Hong Kong. In both of these places, streetcar riding had special associations for me; for once, in my youth, while riding back and forth to work on streetcars in Toronto, I read the entire Bible, starting with "In the beginning" one November day when the snow was sifting against the windows like salt, and reaching "Amen" the following August, when the elms were swooning to the sound of cicadas. It all came back to me in Hong Kong and in Kyoto, where I often rode streetcars right after reading the teachings of Buddha, which you find in hotels there along with, or instead of, the Bible. There's nothing like riding a streetcar for meditation and quiet contemplation of the human race.

For one thing, there are all kinds of illustrations of scripture happening around you. One frosty morning I saw an old monk hurrying across a temple courtyard, late for work, rustling through the fallen leaves of the ginko trees, as if he'd forgotten something, and that happened right after I'd been reading about Buddha asking, on seeing an old man, "Why is that man suffering?" and being told by his charioteer, "That is old age, my lord, it's the ruination of memory"—I think.

There were scenes hard to make jibe with scripture, like those composed little Japanese hotel lobbies with all the guest slippers laid out on the front steps beside a rock garden and small waterfall. There was no sign of the guests, who were still asleep, probably still pink from their hot baths and rub-down and sake and geisha girls, and not up to pondering "All suffering stems from craving the pleasures of life."

Kyoto started the first public streetcar line in Japan in January 1895, and used to have the splendid custom of employing teen-age boys in bright coats called *happi* coats to run ahead of the car shouting at people to get out of the way, and sometimes getting hit themselves until the authorities installed a device on the streetcar called a "boy catcher." But today Kyoto city hall is fighting to do away with streetcars altogether and I, for one, hope they lose.

In Hong Kong, streetcars are comfortable, rattling, congenial double-deckers. But there I got the strong feeling that man doesn't take the fine ideas from his holy books to work with him, the same feeling I used to get when in Toronto I'd look up from reading, say, "Blessed are the meek for they shall inherit the earth," to see twenty-five people shouldering one another out of the way to get on at Sherbourne Street. A Chinese

conductor, who supposedly believed, along with Buddha, "Respect the self of your fellow man as you respect
your own," looked at me just like an Avenue Road bus
driver, as if thinking, "*He* can speak Chinese all right,
when he wants to." A little old lady in black pants who
boarded at Ice House Street, but who might have got
on at Broadview Avenue, looked at me as if she didn't
trust anyone with those sneaky round eyes, and thought
that I probably stuck needles into Chinese girls and
carried them off to some remote, sinful exotic place like
Hamilton, Ontario.

Outside, in the cold light of dawn, tough-looking
black-bearded Indians stood in front of stores with
guns, looking as if they'd think about things like "Let
man overcome anger by love" next time they visited a
temple, but not before. At Cat Street, five Chinese girls
got on. A Chinese girl is so beautiful you just sit there
staring at her, hypnotized by her face until you just
gradually fall forward and take a high-dive into the
infinite depths of her eyes like a stoned pigeon. These,
who might have just finished reading "Shame on him
that strikes back," all started talking about a girl friend
who wasn't there (I don't speak Chinese but I understand girls, and facial expressions), sounding just like
five girls on their way to work, or on their way home
from work anywhere in the world. I was fascinated by
one lively, pretty girl who, when she relayed what *she*
had said, spoke calmly, quietly, reasonably. When she
reported what the *other* girl had said, she gave an
imitation of someone sort of dim-witted and confused
and dull-voiced, staring straight ahead, stupidly, mouth
hanging open a bit.

One of the many enlightened ideas of the Hong Kong
Tourist Association is to publish diagrams of walks you

can take around the city, and the Information Bureau of Macau, an old Portuguese colony on an estuary of the Canton River, reached from Hong Kong by hydrofoil or ferry, outlines tours you can make by bus, pedicab or bike, but I recommend an even slower way—walking. Here, as in Hong Kong, the waterfront is a weaving, bobbing, waving conglomeration of masts and washing, rope, corrugated tin, reed mats, potted plants, dogs, cats, kids, bamboo poles, drying fish, poultry baskets, tubs and crowing roosters. You see the skipper of a junk that is festooned with old tires, easing his craft out to sea, doing it in little movements, waiting for the motion of the water to relax the grip of the tires, just keeping enough pressure on. Now and then a tire pops up in the air like a tiddlywink. On the quay three supple-waisted housewives face the sea doing a kind of calisthenics, arching their backs, doing knee bends and graceful ballet-like motions with limp arms, kicking languidly.

Hong Kong is one of the most crowded areas on earth, with people crammed together 300,000 to a square mile in some areas. Yet on one of my walks I came across a fair where about 10,000—or 100,000—Chinese and myself deliberately jammed ourselves in even tighter. There's something relaxing about submerging into a crowd, like sinking into a warm tub. We shuffled through the hot, dusty grounds taking steps half an inch long, raising such a haze that people held their handkerchiefs over mouths and noses, leaving visible only their eyes—and all the eyes had an expression of fascinated alarm. A cop passed the Goh Fung Shoe display with the fingers of one white-gloved hand splayed over his face, as if we were all being

attacked by nerve gas, which, in a way, we were, except
that it was more like laughing gas.

Signs posted on the booths said if someone picked
your pockets to stand still and yell. You could hardly
move your arms enough to pick anyone's pocket, let
alone make your getaway afterward. All the while, a
woman's voice, amplified to the volume of jet aircraft,
belted out a warm, ribald tune—something between a
football yell and strip music—from the Fung Hang
Record booth. It beat down on us with a strange
anaesthetizing effect, like being shaken by a lion. Kids
yelled, clung to little merry-go-round carts grimly, and
flaked out on their father's shoulders. Old men spat.
Nothing discouraged us. Once we all squeezed like
refugees into an empty building display, and came out
the other side still half convinced that something wonderful had happened in there but we just hadn't been
able to see it. Within a distance of an overpass from
Hong Kong's enormous shopping districts (there are
236 air-conditioned shops in one complex alone), which
include boutiques with names like "Brigitte" and
"Christine," women struggled nearly out of their bra
straps to buy Tin Shing Cosmetics and I fought my
way to buy a transistor radio I didn't want, for $4.00,
shoving my way toward a cheerful, smiling girl who
strained toward me holding the radio out to me over
the crowd's heads, as if it was a life preserver and we
were all drowning. We all passed up those deadly
serious displays of things like floor coverings and bridal
gowns, but crowded around a space the size of a prayer
rug near the Hua Yip Wig display to watch a youth
with a flushed, proud, pleasantly lumpy face, punching one of those bags that rate your punching power
on a dial, putting his shoulder into it, steadying the

ball, then springing at it like a frenzied cat. We wandered around eating bright orange chicken feet, hot lychee nuts, baked plovers' eggs, steamed wieners wrapped in waffles, cotton candy, ice cream cones, lobster-and-egg wafers, and wearing that expression of privilege and bliss people get when they eat standing up, outdoors. We forgot the marvels of medical science, and even acupuncture, to buy little tubes of stuff which, according to the label, was good for "filthy gases poisoning, chill and fever, cold and influenza, dizziness and headache, travel sickness, lumbago, alcoholic leg pains, abrasions, unspecified tumour, toothache, stroke and snake bite," a few drops of which you could also apply to children, although it didn't say what would happen: for all you knew they'd disappear. The big thing was you could buy two tubes for the price of one.

We all had that pleasant feeling of being at the real source of things, and as the crowd eased a bit at dusk, we strolled around eating ice cream cones while the breeze from the harbour gently lifted the discarded wrappers. We all hated to leave this warm and tattered tent of life, noise and experience, convinced that something indescribably exciting was going to happen within the next few minutes, and we sniffed appreciatively at the sea, which was giving off the special smell of salt, iodine, boat terminals and fish. A family got out their chopsticks, crouched in a quieter spot (about where the exhibit of caged raccoons and porcupines would be at a fair back home) and started to have a picnic. The girl on the record was still pranging out her song, which I found myself humming. I felt great, and right at home.

Picking Your Own Hotel
and Taking Your Chances

For every tourist living out of bags for six weeks or
so, there comes a time when he begins furtively sniffing
at his sleeves to make sure that it's really quaint 600-
year-old cobbled streets he keeps smelling. If he has an
urge to spend a night at a big modern hotel, you can't
blame him. But to stay at hotels like this all the way
means missing a lot of the best moments of travel.

For one thing, big modern hotels deliberately try to
shut out the city, and in effect shut out the people you
came to see. ("When you're in a strange country, it's
good to see a familiar face," reads a heading on a current ad for Holiday Inns in Europe.) Picking your own
hotel on the spot and taking your chances means that
at least you get a hotel that really belongs to the city,
usually with a moody, intimate view out the window
of street life—little squares, sidewalk cafés and pornog-
raphy shops close enough to hit with a hard bread
roll. You can lean on the window inhaling the fragrance
of food, beer, perfume, cigarettes and canal water, with
the sound of a nightclub band wafting toward you
from a distant bar. There's a view of a rooftop
weather vane—a rusty metal sailing ship scudding

across a cloudy sky under full sail, off for Van Deimen's Land or the West Indies—and reflections of houses dangling upside down in green water flecked with golden leaves. A prostitute strolls along the kerb with her poodle, looks up and sticks her tongue out at you, sensing that you're the enemy, a happily married man in bed for the night.

Whoever wrote that ad about it being good to see a familiar face in a strange country has the right idea but the wrong people. I have more in common with, say, a Greek desk clerk who stands smiling at his desk and perspiring and hoping things will turn out all right while everything falls apart around him—reservations, plumbing systems, chairs—than with successful tourists from my home town staying at a Holiday Inn. And although nobody can deny that a big room with warm beds is a luxury, they often go with cold people. I prefer one of those Dutch rooms the size of a walk-in closet that you reach up a stairway like an upholstered ladder—that's the sort of place where you really appreciate the little kind gestures of the people who run the hotel, who give you the feeling that you're all in this together; for instance, when a husky smiling Dutch maid six feet high comes in and finds you sitting on the edge of the bed with your knees touching the wall, sulking, looks down at you with a friendly smile, picks up your bag that weighs as much as a power mower and shoots it up on top of a wardrobe to show you how you can make more room for yourself —and then beams down at you as if she'd be glad to throw you up there, too, if it would help.

I've seen more familiar faces in bad hotels that I've picked myself than I've ever seen around hotels with doormen and taxi lines, like the time I looked down from a hotel window in Greece and saw three men sitting in the outer office of the Aphrodite Advertising Agency. While I watched, they all started to sing in harmony. It was a sight and sound I'll never forget, as if three advertising salesmen sitting in the foyer of J. Walter Thompson suddenly all started to sing "Down by the Old Mill Stream." I felt that I knew them immediately. It made me think of the years when I was in advertising, and the many hours that I had spent waiting for brisk young space buyers, trying to keep my mind from wandering onto something else and to convince myself that making a sale was really important.

It's true that by not making reservations at good hotels you run the risk not only of getting a bad one, but of not getting a room for the night at all, but even this puts you in touch with the familiar faces of people who bungle through life coping the best they can—people like clerks and students and civil engineers who are genuine travellers, on their way here and there on various missions, keeping their thoughts to themselves. One time my wife and I couldn't find a room and had to sleep on reclining chairs in a sort of flop-house above a railway station, a strange experience of being in the thick of things, with people I couldn't see in the dark, coming and going. The railway clerk who ran this operation, presumably as a side-line, was a cheerful man who marked down the time people wanted to be awakened, and was as good as his word. At various times during the night you'd see him standing there in a beam of light in the doorway giving someone in our room a call, and there'd be strange sounds of comings and goings and of pants dropping and being pulled on, and quiet curses. When we first lay down there were five men and one woman arranged around a room that became pitch black as soon as the clerk closed the door. When we woke up, there were two women and one man, me. One woman was still there as my wife and I got up, shook ourselves and caught our train through the misty countryside.

18

"We Loved Spain,
But We Couldn't Stand France"

Anyone planning a trip today faces the question of whether to sign up for an organized guided tour (there are hundreds, specializing in all sorts of things, from tours of castles to visits to beer gardens) or just to plan things himself as he goes along, or to avoid planning anything at all, which for my money is the only way to travel.

I don't mean because the people in tour groups are unworldly and as folksy as strawberry jam and completely unlike those tall slender people who appear in the travel ads, drinking Drambuie by Greek moonlight. I like the people you meet on tours, and I don't like those people in the ads, who can't fool me: they're Rotarians under those continental jackets. But it's a mistake to travel in groups, on a planned schedule. For one thing, organized tours are based on the assumption that you'll feel like, say, looking at Great Spanish Art, at precisely eleven o'clock on Tuesday. The odds on this, I've found, are about the same as on your winning a new car with a box top. I remember the first time I saw Notre Dame Cathedral I joined my group outside the entrance on schedule right after I'd had a fight with a taxi driver, who took his tip before he gave me my change. All within sixty seconds I pounded the top of a cab and tried to look up "I'll have you arrested, you French bastard," in a phrase book—and then stood looking at naves and arches. To this day I remember walking through that magnificent historic symbol of Christian love and understanding filled with thoughts of jumping up and down on a cab driver's stomach, or challenging him to a duel, or both, which is not the way to absorb the beauty of great architecture.

But even if you're in the mood, it's impossible to get fifty other people all in the same mood and thinking of the same thing at the same time, and just noticing your tour mates, or even trying not to notice them, can be distracting, to put it mildly. Once, in the Rijksmuseum in Amsterdam my thoughts were completely distracted from the guide's explanations of Vermeer's handling of light and shadow by the technique of the mother of a kid who had whipped around and whispered fiercely to his sister, "If—you—shove—me—once—more!" His mother just reached around and took a swing at both of them without taking her eyes off great art. At the same time a teen-age girl said to her father, a big man in a blue windbreaker with a camera lashed across his chest, "I wish you'd just *try* to understand—*just once.*" I remember his bending his head and saying dryly: "I'm all ears," looking at his toes, as if he'd had it with teen-age daughters, art and Europe. Then we all moved off to look at some Rembrandts, although I'm not quite sure why. For all the culture we were picking up we could all have been in Poughkeepsie shooting a few games of pool.

The basic idea of getting together a lot of strangers,

all of whom have different tastes, temperaments, backgrounds and ideas, and abruptly taking them through fifty rooms of art before lunch, ignores a lot of things, like the nature of man, and even the nature of art. And it doesn't work any better to lead them across famous ancient ruins. Some of the most famous ancient ruins are, on the surface, not much different than a broken-down stone silo in a hot field. They mean something to a scholar—a student of archaeology, for instance, who has been studying them for five years in fat textbooks until he knows where every clay pot was found, and who found it, and what it represented in the march of man's technology. He approaches a site like this with the same sort of feeling that a kid who has been playing hockey in his back yard in North Bay has when he first sees the Montreal Canadiens play the Boston Bruins.

But most of us think of old ruins about as often as we have our teeth examined, if as often, and it's an entirely different matter to suddenly turn some old gent loose on, say, the site of Mycenae on a hot day. He just looks as if he's been abandoned, maybe to die, and he stands looking at urns wondering when the tour will end. He's apt to react like one nice old gent I remember from Kincardine, Ontario (folks up around his way pronounce it King-car-DEEN, with a brisk rhythm, like a spring crick). We had been shown the foundations of a 3,000-year-old town, then taken into a museum to watch a demonstration of ancient pottery making given by a girl in blue jeans and moccasins, and when she had drawn the neck of a jar up with a caress of her thin delicate fingers the man said, by gollies, that reminded him of a bird-feeder they had back at home, back of the snowball bush, and did she know if that was the same kind of clay they got back in

"Kingcardeen," and the girl just squashed her pot with her fist to signal that the demonstration was over and went to a corner of the room and sat on the floor and rolled a cigarette, leaving us all kind of closing in around the old gent to let him know that we were on his side and thought the girl was very rude. On that same historic site I walked behind a thin woman from Ottawa with a big wide black hat, who, as we clambered over the floor of somebody's palace, stopped now and then to discuss something with a big stout pink-faced smiling woman companion. As I'd seen her now and then making notes of the guide's remarks, I figured she was commenting on some fine points of the restoration of the palace and was curious to hear what they were; but when I got close to her I heard her say, "Well, if you ask me, if George marries her it serves him right; he's drunk so much, it's softened his brain," obviously thinking George was more fascinating than 3,000-year-old storehouses for wine, and she was probably right.

The world is full of marvellous things, but the belief that life will be incomplete for anyone who doesn't see them all is a conviction held by some of the unlikeliest people. I know women who, all their lives, have been able to walk past art galleries, museums and cathedrals in their own home towns without even knowing they were there, but who suddenly start saying that they can't die happy without seeing the Parthenon. I've watched men who have never thought of anything more aesthetic than how to recognize a Communist by his haircut, in all practical matters, use the word "intellectual" as a synonym for "traitor," suddenly claim that they feel they owe it to themselves to see the spires of Oxford.

I don't believe any of them. I think they're just combining the fad of world travel with the peculiar faith in culture that we all cling to, like a lingering faith in all-wool socks. It comes out in some odd demonstrations of snobbery, like the example I once saw on a tour bus near Argos in Greece. Right after the guide's lecture, which ended with her reading, ". . . so now I am still awatch for the signal flame, the gleaming fire that is to harbinger news from Troy and tidings of its capture. For thus rules my Queen, woman in sanguine heart and man in strength and purpose . . ." we boarded the bus, drove a way, and stopped to buy some oranges from a roadside farmer, who stood beside the road, on a drowsy, beautiful evening and who weighed them out on an ancient set of hand scales. Right in the middle of it the voice of a woman from Chicago cut across the still evening air like the slap of a wet fish on a butcher's block "Kilos! Kilos! What's all this about kilos? Gimme a dozen oranges." She evidently thought kilos were some kind of trick, like the clause in small type on a used-car contract; but what fascinated me was the way we all sat in the bus staring straight ahead and looking pleased, as if we all read Homer in the original Greek. It was clearly the most interesting thing that had happened to us since we'd had our last beer, and if I were operating a tour I'd plant someone like that woman on every bus to make insensitive remarks that people could take back home for souvenirs, like hand-woven tablecloths.

Yet the Greece of the present, which surrounds its ancient ruins, is there for everyone to enjoy. It's still one of the few places left on earth where you still find spontaneity, joy and warm communication between human beings, and all this is given special significance by the fact that it still goes on in spite of, and sometimes in defiance of, a government of bullyboys. Men still dance simply because they feel like dancing, sing at the helms of fishing boats, and live with such zest that a visit to Greece is like being dropped on to another planet. The relaxed life is partly due to the sunny climate. The sea is warm and as clear as gin. A man will go out in the evening for a swim with his dog, the two floating along a quarter mile offshore like corks.

Much of the life in Greece takes place outdoors. Restaurant owners set tables on the sidewalk and, if they need more space, right on out onto the street. In some towns, like Patras, the street is barricaded so cars won't annoy the diners. People parade languidly up and down the white moonlit streets and the voices of village children playing games in the soft Aegean nights is one of the memorable sounds of Greece.

Strolling through these places in the evening is like being in a village under some kind of enchantment. You hear music, look in a doorway of a café and see a man alone in shirt sleeves, doing a poised and intricate dance among the tables. He waves and invites you to join him.

Families dine at tables laid with white tablecloths in a town square under a fountain-shaped street lamp. Children play around the tables; there is quiet conversation, the clink of wine glasses. The children scuttle among parents' and grandparents' legs at all hours, thoroughly loved and knee-deep in approval. The process of going to bed apparently stretches out indefinitely. You hear a child's laugh somewhere above you at ten in the evening and look up and catch a glimpse of a bare-bellied youngster being chased around a balcony by a doting grandmother. I asked one Greek

woman if they had sitters in Greece. She didn't know
what I meant. When I explained that a sitter was someone who looked after the children when you went out
to have a good time, she looked at me, appalled. In
Greece you take the children with you to have a good
time.

Parents seem to take a special pride in dressing their
children. You walk up a street that looks like a social-
worker's nightmare, and out of a dark and squalid
doorway comes a little girl in an immaculate dress so
white you'd think she was standing in a spotlight.

Greeks express human emotions that give you new
feelings about belonging to the human race. Customers
stand around staring at you if you're, say, buying a pair
of running shoes, until you wonder if you've violated
some local taboo, then suddenly one will bend down
and feel to see if your toes come to the end of the
shoes, and you realize she's really concerned about
their being too short and giving you ingrown toenails.
One time a woman came out of a shop when my wife
and I were trying to buy some film without being able
to make ourselves understood. She nodded, smiled
vigorously and sent someone across the road for a
friend who spoke English. While we waited, she
brought out a worn and backless kitchen chair for my
wife to sit on, dusted it off, blew on it and motioned to
her to sit down, and then stood beaming at us to indi-
cate she couldn't have been happier about our being
there—although she hadn't the faintest idea what we
wanted. Another time when we wandered around a
maze of silent, narrow back streets of a town that wandered up a hillside, admiring the flowers that blazed
against the white stone walls, a woman in a black head
kerchief came hustling out of a house toward us,

grasped our hands and smiled in a spontaneous personal welcome to Greece. Greek people act without hesitation on impulses of goodwill. Once, up in the hills, a man whom we'd turned down as a guide came running after us and handed my wife a flower to show there were no hard feelings.

Meeting people like that is a lot better than visiting old ruins, but it's impossible to plan them on guided tours. For guided tours shield the visitor from the natives and protect him from experience, which should be the whole object of travel. I read an ad the other day for a ten-day tour of Britain that said, "See a genuine British pub." You don't "see" a British pub, you feel it, and when you're alone and unprotected it can be like a death ray. The longest walk I've ever taken was across twenty feet of faded oriental rug between me and a pair of French doors, which was the escape route from one cosy little pub I dropped into on a rainy night, and stood looking at a fire in a grate and listening to the throat-gulping silence around me, and feeling the texture of old friendships, as thick as Yorkshire pudding. The only sound I heard was a whisper from the woman behind the bar who said something to a stocky man in a brown jacket with a bull terrier, and called him "dear," like Aunt Anne soothing Timothy Forsyte when finding out that someone had upset him. I felt like a bounder, a travel experience that you can't show back home on color slides, along with the Changing of the Guard.

It wouldn't have happened, or rather, wouldn't have penetrated to me, if I'd been with a group; even if it had, I could have camouflaged a casual retreat, and later joined the ranks of tourists who make quick and final judgements about whole areas of the earth with

those summaries like—"We loved Spain but we couldn't
stand France." But on your own, you just don't leave
a place that quickly and completely.

As it was, I was stuck there in the hotel, my wife already in our room for the night, and I figured that
since I was already a cad I might as well make some
more notes. So I went downstairs to another lounge
and tested the theory of an English friend of mine who
had told me that an Englishman's reserve is really shy-
ness. "Talk to these people," he said. "They don't talk
to strangers because strangers don't talk to them." I
deliberately picked a couple who sat by a window, the
man with his fingers splayed against his face as if he
was protecting himself from the glances of visitors, and
I made a remark about the coffee being hot and I
wished my bedroom were that warm.

There was an instant of shock. The man and his
wife looked at me aghast. Then the man asked me
where I was from, and I said Canada, and he said I
was right about the coffee and he wished they'd put it
in hot-water bottles in the beds, which was all the
bloody stuff was good for and he envied me coming
from Canada, where he'd heard they had an ingenious
idea for coping with cold weather, they built fires.

I later told a friend of mine about my experience—a
little guy about five foot four I'd worked with for years
who originally came from England, but so long ago
he'd lost most of his accent—and he told me of *his* experience in an English pub. Not only did the people
ignore him, but one man kept doing sly little imitations
of what he considered to be an American accent, until
something in my friend snapped and he stood in the
middle of the room, all five foot four of him, and made
the pronouncement that he'd been born in Sandy Patch

not ten miles away and for twenty years he'd been looking forward to seeing England again and now that he had, he'd like to make the official announcement that he was ashamed to be an Englishman; upon which a tall Englishman with a beard came over and asked him if he'd accept his apologies for the whole bloody roomful of English and be his guest next morning at Buckingham Palace, where he was some kind of secretary. The next day he gave him a great private tour, during which my friend caught a glimpse of the Queen flitting across a corridor, looking very informal and domestic as if, maybe, she'd decided to make herself a piece of toast before facing her loyal subjects that day.

"My Charter Flight Was Terrible,
and Next Year's Will Probably Be Worse"

Today's traveller has to make more adjustments to his environment than Stanley and Livingstone. Not physically—apart from passing through time zones and customs line-ups and being frisked, he doesn't go through anything different crossing the polar ice cap than he does sitting at home watching "Mannix." But he has to adjust psychologically to losing romantic ideas that have sustained ordinary folk for generations. I mean ideas like the subtle delights of travel snobbery, for instance—of some day being able to travel when others can't. It's amazing how the notion that travel is a rare reward lingers on. Crooks on TV programs still put off their girl friends, who are begging them to stop before it's too late ("We'll go away somewhere, just you and me") by saying, just this one more job, honey, trust me, then—the guy paints an irresistible picture—Spain! France! The Riviera!—ignoring the fact that hundreds of thousands of people, including high-school kids, are going to these places without holding up banks, or even interrupting their education.

Today's traveller has to learn to abandon the notion that he's one of a lucky elite. Instead, he should sit

back, put on his travel slippers and enjoy mingling
with his fellow man in large groups, and there's no
better place to do it than on a charter flight. Some people still try to recapture a bit of the old joys of snobbery by travelling first-class, but it doesn't come off.
Travelling first-class on a plane where 180 other people
back there are wedged in three abreast in wrinkled
clothes is like trying to bring back fox hunting by rop-
ing off half a dozen lots in a low-cost housing development for a chase.

I travelled first-class a few times in my life and enjoyed all the service, but found on one trip that up
there in front of those curtains there was a small, for-
lorn class system, in which, incidentally, I was at the
bottom of the scale. I didn't feel like drinking or calling
strangers by their first names, which the others were
all doing. They were able to spot a loner like a drop in
interest rates and were soon ignoring me, except to
glance over occasionally as if I were a dangerous radi-
cal. The only time I was included in the conversation
was when I wanted to find out something about ground
transportation and asked the steward the best way to
get to Toronto. At that point a man from Vancouver,
under the strange compulsion of people from that city,
came over to my seat, told me there was no good way
to get to Toronto, and went back to talking to a man
called Harry, having carried out this strange West
Coast ritual. Otherwise it was a club, and as anachro-
nistic as a college snake dance.

But the people who sit aft of the curtain are by and
large free of guff, and they're at their best on a charter
flight, when they reveal how friendly mankind can be
when he's taking three weeks off from work. In airports
they wander around in green cardigans and mackin-

toshes that Wernher Von Braun couldn't get the wrin-
kels out of, whistling Scottish tunes, and looking as if
they just came in from raking last summer's asters, or
from a fishing trip. Usually they carry things they
brought back from the old country—family heirlooms,
smoked meats, candies, hammered brass coal boxes, jars
of strawberry jam, Irish blackthorn walking sticks, and
they're surrounded by so many shopping bags that they
look as if they'd all just come out of the A&P. They
press together in untidy little groups for psychological
warmth, wearing badges and making remarks that give
a strong feeling of family ties, like "If we could only
get Mum and Dad out here," and exchange strange
remarks over the heads of the crowd. "Where's Jamie?"
I once heard a voice from a crowd of greeters call.
"I've no idea," another voice answered from the customs door. "We came over Greenland."

They're as refreshing and reassuring as a nice hot
cup of tea after those cold globe-trotting characters in
the travel ads. They work their way across airport floors
amid mounds of luggage looking as if they'd floated
across the ocean on them, like Thor Heyerdahl, making
cheerful remarks like "One more mile," not quite sure
what they flew over but talking about new sons-in-law
and daughters-in-law they finally got a chance to meet.
Between planes they collapse in tired groups as if
they'd been swept there with push brooms, along with
a lot of straw hats and babies in pink sleepers lying
belly-down on baggage like stuffed toys. They're as far
as you can get from self-consciously blasé businessmen
who march onto airplanes all carrying the same attaché case, smelling of Brut, fly over mountains, lakes
and forests without looking up from data sheets on pipe

fittings, then all get up and try to beat everyone else off the plane without speaking.

Charter-flight passengers sing songs like "Glasgow Belongs to Me," play bingo, sometimes play the bagpipes, make funny personal announcements about their fellow passengers over the public address system that would make stuffier travellers sue someone, give three cheers for the captain when he lands the plane, and they often get so sentimental about seeing England or Scotland or Ireland or Italy or their grandchildren that they arrive tight and have to be wheeled onto the old sod in wheelchairs.

A traveller on a charter flight meets a lot of warm, genuine people. Although they may not look distinguished, they look as if they may manage to pull the world closer together. While distinguished-looking statesmen with compelling voices are trying to outfox one another at peace talks, insulting one another in several languages at the United Nations and exchanging guns with friendly nations, ordinary people on charter flights are making friends with people in other countries, inviting one another to return visits, communicating by smiles and drawings, shouting cheerfully at one another in their mother tongues and exchanging things like teapots and old magazines. They're apt to be emotional when they meet members of the family, and grandmothers, oblivious of the crowds and bedlam of airports, lean over to tie kids' shoelaces, button coats, tighten scarfs—anything to get as close to their grandchildren as possible and *touch* them.

Charter-flight passengers are apt to be less concerned with what Jason did with the golden fleece than with where Mom put the strawberry jam, but they exhibit the classic emotions of mankind. Once I saw a cold, tall, distinguished Englishman who looked as if he owned six railways and a bank arrive off a plane to be greeted by a swarm of relatives. He looked down with very little expression at his new daughter-in-law, who suddenly reached up and kissed him. He accepted this apparently without feeling and probably would have gotten away with it but a woman his age, whom I judged to be his sister, suddenly stared at him in surprise and said, "You're *trembling!*"

I can still see the faces of some people I've met on charter flights a lot more clearly than I can see some castles I've visited. One belonged to a Scottish woman with that rare kind of beauty in which sheer love and gentleness toward mankind shine through a face as plain as a pumpkin, who told me that the year before she had travelled as a member of a cattle breeders' association, a musical appreciation group, and a skiing club, all the members of which were apparently going to use the same skis, as there was only one pair on the plane. She insisted on holding my brief case and topcoat on her lap while I walked around the airport making some notes. An hour later, when I suddenly remembered I'd left them with her, she was still holding them, saying it didn't matter a bit, and looking as if she would have held me on her lap too, if it was the only way I could get a seat.

The charter flight has made it possible for many of these people to travel for the first time in their lives, or to get back to see the old country again after a lapse of twenty, twenty-five years. It's not hard to understand the attitude of one woman I talked to, in charge of charter flights for a big company, who sat among jars of Coffee-mate, postcards, world maps, potted plants and travel posters, and told me her philosophy about charter flights. She said the government could make any regulations it liked, but any time some elderly couple came to her whose family had left them alone with nothing but their arthritis and who wanted to see Ireland again, she was going to see that they got on a plane, even if she had to swear that the applicants had both been members of a Polish weight-lifters' club for six months, and the government could put her in jail if they wanted to.

Charter flights may emerge from the thick fog that governments and major organizations have created by making what became known as the "affinity rule," (meaning the passengers had to have an affinity for something, like bowling). One major airline put out a folder to help clear up the confusion and some of the answers to questions are hard to believe. Question: "What kind of organizations travel at charter rates?" Answer: Almost any kind of organization, unless it was formed from the general public for the principal purpose of obtaining low-cost air transportation. . . ."

Some of these flights probably do more toward creating a wholesome confusion about the difference in races than the United Nations. Stewardesses who can give instructions on how to survive at sea in tones that sound as if you've been chosen runner-up in a Miss Orange Grove Contest, suddenly find themselves involved with raw emotions and fierce family love. They get their hair in their eyes and their blouses come out as they try to cope with people who get up to the crow of roosters and the sound of oarlocks. A lot of them are ready to quit after a Greek charter made up of villagers whose idea of the modern bathroom is one with ridges on those treadles you grip with your feet over a hole in the ground. They explain to baffled little women from the hills that what you do with a toilet is get on it—and they find them standing on it. Sometimes they arrive in North America with the five washrooms of a super jet all abandoned, and the only clean part of the plane forward of the flight-deck door. But there's a lot of warmth and friendship on the cabin side of it, and I've talked to stewardesses who suddenly stop describing the chaos to look thoughtful about the way old Greek women reached up and stroked their hair with affection when all they did was bring them four cups of coffee.

There's no doubt that charter flights often seem casually organized. Sometimes there are long delays. One woman told me of being in Reykjavík airport for thirty-six hours, a delay so long that some of the younger passengers started to put in the time by finishing up their marijuana, with older folks going around sniffing curiously, figuring they were getting the scent of a kind of lichen that grew in the far North. Charter-flight passengers enjoy exaggerating tales of breakdowns and diversions, making it all sound more adventuresome. Often when you ask them how the trip went they'll say something like "ghastly," then tell you of the three they were on in previous years, which were terrible, and the one they're going on next year, which will probably be worse. As one friend of mine, a veteran department-store charter-flight passenger, put it, "You'd be surprised at how close it makes you feel to people you work with." He stopped to wave to a girl in the silverware department. "I don't know her name, but you feel you've been through something together."

Wanted—A Nice
New Old-fashioned Place to Visit

One result of today's rapid communication of ideas is that all cities are beginning to look the same. Soon there will be no point in visiting them unless chambers of commerce and city councils start thinking up bold new plans, like leaving their cities alone. Any city council who adopted this plan would have something different from everything that lies between Brasília and Brampton, Ontario. Politicians could get up and say, "At the present moment in time, we propose doing nothing to attract visitors," and sit down—to watch millions of people rolling in to see the city.

A tourist would be glad to escape there from the new spectacular hotels with lobbies like broadloomed sections of the Grand Canyon and guests sitting around so far apart that they can't hear what one another are saying.

By contrast I struck a great old-time lobby the other day where a group from the North of England who were in town for a Holstein breeders' tour, had gathered. I sat there listening to them, pretending I was dozing. (Pretending, the great game of tourists, was more exciting in the old hotels, where you were under closer observation by fellow guests—you could look mysterious and interesting. For all the other guests knew, you might be an unfrocked bishop or a Mediterranean duke, or a mining tycoon with three homes and a yacht.) One man behind me was telling a couple of tour mates about some "steady lass who had been seeing a lad with a head on his shoulders who wanted to marry her, but there was another bloody daft lad she liked better," and he thought if the lass had any sense she'd "bloody well wait till she was twenty-seven to get married anyway, because a lad married at eighteen was likely to bloody well start rambling by the time he was twenty-one, sowing his wild oats." It was an enchanting moment. I sat there thinking of murky North of England farms and a lass with a head on her shoulders sitting peering out of a thatched cottage window at some Holsteins, dreaming of the bloody daft lad.

Hotels should also have old-fashioned bathtubs with thin sides that boom when you hit them with your knee. The tubs should hold enough hot water to let you float in them without the water starting to drain out before your horrified eyes through those mean little holes about eight inches above the bottom, and they should have rolled edges two and a half inches wide that you can get a grip on without having to have a hand like Joe Namath. Incidentally, the two-and-a-half-inches-wide design is an old-fashioned one that was recently voted the most efficient devised by man by a group of experts who were investigating why plumbing manufacturers persist in making rectangular tubs when there are still no rectangular people.)

There should be an annual award for hotel owners who resist trying to dazzle tourists with impressive bbies and, instead, offer little services like wrapping up your packages or repairing the handles on luggage. Even better, they should run shops that will press a tourist's pants while he waits. This would be a particularly appreciated service for men like me who resist the new crease-resisting knit fabrics that feel as if you've shoved your legs through the sleeves of a pullover and who stick to the old-fashioned comfortable smooth fabrics. These wrinkle like leaves and have to be pressed often. But this provides a pleasant interlude in a dry cleaning shop when someone motions for you to go into a booth at the rear, indicating that you're to take your pants off and hand them out through the door. You sit there in a relaxed steamy atmosphere, peering out from a rain forest of dangling garments, like a shy threatened woodland creature, rearranging things in your billfold, counting your money, seeing how many pencils you have collected in your pockets and having the pleasure of discovering an old cigarette butt in your pocket that you had put aside for tough times and forgotten about, then taking your pants from a detached hand that appears around the door and stepping out into the afternoon sunlight in tune with nature, where things gradually get more wrinkled, then, with heat and moisture, sprout again full of new life and hope.

The only kind of $60-million developments that would be encouraged in the sensible City of Tomorrow would be complexes designed to duplicate exactly the old part of the city that had been torn down, with pawn shops and old buildings with worn wooden stairways that will suit the tourist's mood on mornings when he can't face things like the world's highest archway, or the Olympic Games, or bright lights or progressive people. There would be lots of second-hand junk stores and old dark movie houses that he can nip into and have a sleep during reshowings of old Westerns, waking up occasionally to the sound of gunfire and Kirk Douglas saying, "We've got good grass in the river bottom and we don't aim to have barbed wire around it."

The New City would have an Old-Shopper's mall with at least one old-time hardware store, the only place left where men can get away from women. A tourist, up to here with art galleries, could go in and heft mallets, grip handles of planes, and make little gouging motions with chisels; he could put hammers on the floor to see if they balanced properly on the claws like rocking chairs, which means the hammer has just the right shape, or gives the satisfying impression that it has just the right shape. He could peer into bins of rope—mountain-climbers' rope and great sacks of hemp hawsers for warping ships—which all men like to look at; and he could avidly read the instructions on the latest preparations for gluing together the things of this life that have become unstuck.

The place would smell of axe handles, paint, oil, nails and putty, and there would be clerks specially trained to listen to a traveller describe some great project he plans to finish when he gets home, following the clerk right behind the counter, past rawhide mallets from England, chisels from Sweden and post-hole diggers. "Tell you what I want her for. I have some flashing come loose around a drop panel, and I've got to cut a hole through a two-inch board and a one-inch board at an angle," he'd say as he disappeared among chains, stillson wrenches, bench vises, bolts, corks and screws, using a jargon women won't catch onto for three more generations, words like grout, hods, shims, cotter pins, dowel pegs, spanners and cantsaw files and second-cut files.

In place of those new drugstores appearing in every city all over the world, with magic-eye gates and shopping carts and 10,000 items all at discount prices, but no clerks, there'd be an old-time quiet, shady, cluttered cave with sagging wooden floors, embossed tin ceiling and an overhead fan that mingled its soft zephyrs with the summer breeze coming in the door and the smell of lilacs, cough drops and licorice. In charge would be an old-time druggist in carpet slippers trailing a faint fragrance of developing fluid, rolling tobacco, chocolates, ice cream and horehound.

A drugstore used to be the most restful place on earth. You could fall asleep there waiting for your prescription to be filled, your life reduced to a few fundamentals, just you, your itch, and a fly buzzing around a window display of trusses. The pharmacist would disappear between a pair of green curtains into his dispensary, a gassy, smelly, exciting place of flames, fumes and brass gram weights, and he'd be away so long you'd figure he'd gone home, or had just decided to take a nap, then you'd hear three taps on a typewriter and know he was back there melting things and looking for keys on the typewriter and coping with your problem.

The city that plays a real part in the tourist world of future will also pay special attention to providing the tourist with plenty of places to sit. Europe has always been far ahead of North America in this. In my own home town, whenever they find people getting overly fond of sitting in one particular place, they pour concrete over it, or fence it off, with a cop at either end checking on the type of sitting they get there. Old treed boulevards, where you could sit on the grass among quietly snoozing prone figures of loafers and failures and come away feeling relatively brisk and successful, are turned as quickly as possible into parking lots and bank buildings. In Europe they've never forgotten the thing that gives progress some point and reason—the individual human being and his peculiar, unchanging human habits. Sitting is an ancient and relaxing art, and in Europe people sit for hours. Young energetic people sit. Middle-aged people sit. Old people and women in mink stoles sit. You don't have to be with anyone to sit. You can just sit there alone and not buy anything, and just turn into a psychological stump for an hour or two, and get up ready to face the world again.

Yet people sitting are at their best (all impassioned speeches are made by people standing up). In the few North American cities where there are still some natural places for people to sit, it's an education just to sit by yourself and look at the other sitters, particularly in northern cities in the spring, when a subtle change comes over people on the first warm bright summery day. For one thing, they stare at their feet as if they haven't seen them since last summer, a sort of stock-taking, like a motorist looking at his tires after a long drive.

They are totally absorbed in anything that's happening around them—a car being parked, a cab driver calling in a friendly, folksy manner to another taxi driver to move up a bit. They sit very still, rarely even tapping a foot or jiggling a leg, and it's probably the only time of year when young men sit as still as old men.

Men of all ages look at passing women with the

same intense concentration, becoming even more motionless, if possible. But old men still wear their hats, while young men take off everything allowed by the law, including their shirts, and, thanks to the new types of footwear, their shoes, which women have been kicking off during relaxed moments for ages. There's a peculiar reflection on earth of what's going on in the heavens during the spring equinox, when day and night are the same length all over the world—a kind of universal balance. The delicate balance seems to be sensed by sitters. People speak in hushed voices, as if being careful not to tip the celestial scales, and they smile to themselves, as if they're momentarily emotionally balanced inside, and they tend to close their eyes. The ideal city would encourage this sort of thing.

Shrewd space-age city tourist organizations will see to it that there will be a small, unprogressive zoo downtown. Cities now all have the biggest zoo in the world, located usually on the outskirts of the city. But zoos should be right downtown with the rest of us who are caught there and can't get out, and it should be small and friendly (a new concept of a community of men and animals all getting along with one another). My ideal zoo would be very practical and educational. The lifeless lines of modern architecture, like today's ghastly office buildings, could be offset by graceful living things like llamas. City hall politicians could be counter-balanced by the composed dignity of old lions, who only roar when they mean it. A young bison would be a reminder of how succeeding generations follow one another in the world of affairs; starting off looking helpless and friendly with two tiny inoffensive-looking horns, wagging its tail a lot, but as soon as it thinks it can succeed, ramming the Old Man, who thought he was in charge forever. The adult male buffalo would be a nice living reminder of how a successful man of affairs, a dictator or revolutionary, gets what he wants; with a head like a battering ram three feet wide, the buffalo just puts it down and runs into anything it doesn't like.

But the main thing about a zoo like this would be that it would provide peaceful, primitive moments as an antidote to crowds and rudeness and the cold contempt of clerks. There's a zoo right near the Seine in Paris. I can remember one evening hearing the peaceful sound of some animal I couldn't see very well—a deer, I think—browsing around some shrubs, and the sound filled me with a great sense of peace and contentment.

I had the same feeling I remembered once when I heard a bull elk, one of a group in an enclosure, feeding in an old apple orchard, giving its peculiar bugling sound as it knocked apples out of a tree with its antlers. It was a wonderful wild busy sound. There'd be the sound of the antlers raking the branches—the elk would squint when he did this, like a man getting his eyebrows trimmed, and listen for the thud of the apples hitting the ground. He ate them noisily. Once he looked under some low branches at a female and stopped chewing, looking at her very thoughtfully.

One of my favorite tourist sites was the zoo in my own home town, which used to be in the centre of the city, but is now being replaced by the biggest zoo in the world in some other town that the city has incorporated. When I was selling advertising I used to drop in at the zoo every now and then between calls and visit some old acquaintances, human and animal. I'd find the director, a pleasant, white-haired pink-faced

Englishman, perhaps walking down one of the shady paths in his shirt sleeves on his way to look at a grizzly with a sore foot. Or I'd meet the zoo foreman and walk over with him to see Abigail the orangoutan, one of the zoo's great thinkers.

"Her wheels go around better than ours," I was told once by the foreman, a man who has studied (and has been studied by) the zoo animals for years.

Abigail worked out a way of slitting a banana peel, leaving the ends intact, so that when she stretched it out it formed a long handy string, with which she could flick things into her cage—popsicle sticks, bits of candy, pieces of paper—that lay beyond her reach outside the bars.

Abigail had weak-looking arms, like those of a lean old man, but she ripped apart old tires that she had been given to play with at the rate of one a month, shredding six-ply nylon cord and reinforced rubber as easily as a woman rips out seams. One time when the director was giving Abigail's ailing husband a shot of penicillin, Abigail, seeing the needle go in, wrapped her arms around the director's legs and threw him to the ground. She gave his leg a good bite, then held him there.

"It was a good-natured hug," said the director, who always stuck up for his animals. He was a husky man, who used to do a lot of rowing, and I asked him if he couldn't pull her arms away. "Oh, no," he said, "her strength is fantastic. She lets go when she wants to let go."

We would stand there while Abigail swung around the cage on her tire, watching her admiringly. She would look out at us admiringly. We'd visit Jane and Charlie the lions, a loving pair who in eight years had forty-three cubs. Lions are good parents, and the male often plays with the cubs. Tigers are different. The male is apt to be too rough with the cubs and the female takes full responsibility for them; females of most species are living hell in a fight with a male.

The zoo was a great place to spend an hour or so after lunch. I remember one time seeing a young man —one of a group of visitors—holding a spider monkey's hand. The monkey was stroking his hand. The director told me, "They love to pet people."

Every future city, then, should have a small downtown zoo, to keep us close to nature. Even better, future tourist associations should shift the emphasis from cities like Las Vegas and Miami and encourage people to visit villages in the county. I mean the sort of village where the visitor can see a general store that is crammed and festooned from embossed tin ceiling to floor with work pants, rake handles, dippers, tea, rubber boots, bush jackets, bucksaws, baseball bats, snow-shoes, washtubs, mops, chinaware—stores that still have old counters with the glass-windowed bins where they used to keep loose salt and cookies, with windows that look out on old barns at the top of hillsides covered with buttercups, spruce woods and waving timothy. Trips will be arranged on trains with courtly gents in blue uniforms standing beside them inclining their heads attentively as you give your destination, touching your elbow to direct you to the right car. Of course, the trains will leave right on schedule, gliding smooth as planets out of stations with a couple of polite toots. As steam passing your window makes the landscape flicker like a light with a loose connection and you glide past creeks and apple orchards, the conductor will come down the aisle taking tickets calmly, thanking the customers, passing down the aisle touching the chair backs as if blessing them.

There'll be special visits to farms, on which groups will stand inside old barns and listen to the wind sigh through the cracks and they'll inhale the great basic fragrances of hay and cow manure, and maybe, with a bit of luck, be able to lean on a sagging barnyard rail with the sun on their heads, listening to a chicken give that slow startled "w-a-a-a-w-w-k!" (a sound better than depth therapy for loosening up tight nerves) as it scratches the earth's surface and peers into it as if looking for its secrets.

Old wooden barns are disappearing from North America. They are being left to fall apart or be stripped by decorators who buy the old weathered planks to use for the interiors of exclusive men's wear stores. But the future tourist on my "Barn Special" will be able to stand around some shadowy old wooden cathedral and have his soul recharged listening to the sound of horses munching, and climb up smooth old wooden steps slippery with hay and festooned with straw dangling from dust webs and stand among bales of clover and sweet grass hearing a loose plank flap in the wind, or a pigeon far up in the ridge make a throaty, doleful lament, or an English sparrow give a distant cheep, as cheerful as ever, after 122 years of the increasing smog and carbon monoxide of man on the move.

The fact is, if the tourist industry is to survive—if the world is to survive, for that matter—we have to change our minds about the meaning of progress. We have to change mayors, too, and get rid of the guys who compete for the tourist trade by bidding for World's Fairs and Disneylands; and get rid of the kind of promoter behind a project I saw advertised the other day. The ad was for a Caribbean resort and it boasted that only a few years ago there hadn't been anything on the island but "two old winter homes and three beautiful beaches." The ad went on to say, "$60 million dollars later we have an island we can call paradise." The place now has a nine-hole golf course, jogging and cycle trails through "sun dappled forests of casuarina trees"—and I, for one, hope it has now collapsed and is overgrown with vines.

~

21

"No Tipping"

I also have some suggestions for basic changes that will have to take place in the travel industry. The practice of tipping should be abolished, although it will probably take a generation to eliminate it. It's one of the most untidy and undignified practices of man and should be eliminated by education, the way everyone is now taught that throwing beer tins on the highway is wrong.

Tipping was started by English and American travellers in the early 1900's with the growth of mass tourism, and it has now reached (I hope) its ultimate state of absurdity. In the travel world, everyone has frankly abandoned any notion that a tip is a generous gesture or a reward for unusually helpful service. I once asked a Frenchwoman in Nice who ran a small hotel what would happen if I didn't tip a waiter and she said he'd explain very politely that I owed him a tip, and go on explaining it all day, or all year, if necessary, and I believe her. A travel agent in, say, New York, will now tell you how much to tip someone 3,000 miles away whom you haven't even met yet, and don't know if you'll like when you do meet him.

I've never been able to hand a grown able-bodied

man a quarter for lifting a bag at an expenditure of energy of about one calorie without feeling that I've insulted him.

Once when my wife and I were crossing the French-Spanish border on our way to Madrid, we got off the train at midnight and joined a long, shuffling line-up of people going through customs and immigration, when a man over six feet tall, in uniform gleaming with braid and epaulets, came up to us. Scattering the natives with a booming voice and a wave of his hand, he took our passports, waved them congenially in the immigration man's face without opening them, said in a jovial roar, "You haven't anything to declare, have you?" and shoved our bags through unopened while the customs men were practically prying open the bread rolls of the other people. Then he escorted us to an empty first-class coach. The whole impression was that some ambassador in Madrid had received word of our arrival. The guy stood outside our open window, looking like Prince Philip; but he seemed to be hesitating, and I asked my wife if she thought he'd run me through with a sword or have me arrested for insulting his country if I offered him a tip. But I took a chance and watched with horror as he saluted smartly, flipped the coin into his trouser pocket, and marched away, very erect. It did something to me, and to Spain, that I'll never quite forget.

It's almost as bad when some guy weighing 250 pounds, with muscles like picnic hams, moves my bag thirty feet to a hotel desk, and when I don't tip him, lifts his hands and lets them flap helplessly at his side as if he's given up trying to stop people taking food out of his children's mouths.

The whole matter of tipping has become so detached from its origins that it has evolved a new kind of language. I remember one head porter in a London hotel, a handsome, youngish man with slight bags under his eyes and a face ruffled into a kind of perpetual smile, who when I didn't tip him (I'd already over-tipped a bellboy so much by accident that he walked away from me stiff-legged as if he'd just been given a fix), went into a peculiar kind of double-talk that, if I interpreted it right, went, "Thank you very *much,* sir, lovetobagcheck for bloodysir nothing or anytime alright up the of course, sir."

I expect to pay for services, but to pay a man is one thing, to hand him a quarter as part of a little game you both play in which you pretend you are grateful for some little service you didn't get, is something else— for instance, when you hand a tip to a cab driver who just sat there listening to a ball game on the radio while you struggled out with your bags. And it's no better in the unlikely case that he really *did* help you with your bags, since your handing him a quarter makes him look as if he's on the very bottom of the labour force, a position comparable, say, to "boots" in an old English inn. Fees should be set, like the cost of butter, and all wages should come from the employer (any employer who lets his employees take part of their wages in tips is, to that extent, not an employer but a con man). Then signs should be posted in airports, railway stations, cab stands and restaurants, saying, "Thank you, but please do not offend our employees by offering them a tip."

The people who have come the closest to working things out are the Japanese. Tipping simply isn't in the air in Japan. When you ask the people at the Japan National Tourist Organization about tipping, they say flatly, "No tipping." You don't tip in trains, or in barbershops or beauty salons, or cabs. If you take a taxi ride and your fare comes to the equivalent of $1.90 and you give the cabbie $2.00, he hurriedly reaches for your dime change. It's all so simple, like buying a package of cigarettes or a pound of tea. In hotels and restaurants, service charge is added to your bill, but that's the end of it. Bellhops grab your bags and don't even wait around hoping you'll forget and tip them again. You begin to get the feeling that they are paid employees whose salary you've helped to pay. It's included in your bill, and that's the way they feel about it too.

22

Language Problems?
Shout Slowly in English

World travel is making people a lot more aware than they used to be of language difficulties and of how everything would be simplified by a universal form of speech to keep pace with universal forms of drugstores, supermarkets, hotels and tourists, but I have a feeling that this would work out less like universal understanding than like a universal income tax or universal toothpaste commercials. I know the first time I saw a Wimpy's restaurant in Amsterdam, conjuring mental pictures of Popeye sitting with his finger in a dike eating spinach, I wanted to take the next plane home. I'd rather we all stuck to the idea that anyone can learn to speak another language, and let ourselves get lured now and then into signing up for courses, with ads like that one showing a little boy with a heading "He can speak Spanish, why can't you?"

The reason he can, of course, is that he spoke it shortly after he was born. I sympathize with anyone who has to communicate in a second language. I loved French class at school, snapping open loose-leaf notebooks, and leafing through new textbooks that squeaked like new shoes, sniffing the glossy pages of vocabularies and slogging with Jean Valjean through rain-soaked idioms and up slippery cobbled alleys of irregular verbs.

But although I could learn the words I could never get the hang of French or any language other than the one I used on Saturday mornings when I was eight, when I asked my mother if I could go camping and waited in an agony of suspense for her to make the right sound, "Yes," a flat, breathy sound that wafted me on my way like a summer zephyr. I can learn words like *oui*, but I can't relate them to certain feelings around the back of my neck or unravel them from the associations with which every word is connected like a tangled kite string. Even facial expressions are important and are caught up in all this. You can smile when you say "yes," for instance, but you can't when you say "no," or "*oui*," which doesn't sound like "yes." It sounds like throwing a quick lasso around a little herd of first-person plurals, and a bit like "wheeee!" which means something entirely different.

But I love listening to another language. I've sat through French movies like *Jules et Jim* two or three times without understanding five words in the whole picture but somehow knowing and understanding the people and their emotions, and I can remember some foreign conversations and pronunciations far more vividly like old tunes than I can remember little historic inscriptions about what Charles the Hammer did in the eighth century. I can still hear the sound of the word "Köbenhàvn" (Copenhagen) pronounced by a girl with red hair, white lipstick and brown eyes on a rainy night as she looked at me slyly from a railway information booth, knowing I could never pronounce it in fifty years; she emitted a kind of low howl, a kind of "koonhown," a wild, tall, Nordic sound bringing visions of campfires on misty shores on the eve of raids. I can remember clearly a long melodious sad monologue by a Mexican youth in a drugstore in Needles, California—a sad, gentle lament, coming right from his soul, although for all I know he may have been telling his pals that the bowling alley was closed on Wednesdays. I can remember the operatic effect of a group of Italian porters in a station restaurant shouting at one another at the top of their lungs, waving their arms and making little gestures, palms up, as if they were lifting sagging shelves. Every now and then, when the noise was almost unbelievable, a fat woman behind a cash desk would stand up and yell, "Eh!" That would cut across the racket like a saber, and all the porters would be quiet for a while—until one would make a motion as if tossing a plate of soup at another and they would all start screaming again.

There's nothing more intriguing for me than watching people communicate perfectly in sounds I don't understand. I once watched a beautiful, oval-faced Italian girl of about sixteen sitting between two women, perhaps her aunts, who were giving her a full barrage of Italian about something, while she sat smiling at the floor, as if she were sitting there alone. Then, slowly, barely perceptibly, she pinched her lips together, stretched up her eyebrows and gave a tiny wiggle of her head, an eloquent universal, mocking gesture, but for me the strange thing was that through that barrage of rapid foreign sounds, the threads of thought had been as simple and clear to her as if the women had simply been saying, "Pass the salt."

But although I love the intricate sounds of other languages, I can't quite get over the conviction that anyone can understand me if I shout slowly, in my own language, calling things by their proper names, like "ham and eggs."

I think it's a mistake to try to turn language into something functional, simple and efficient, like an automatic transmission, with foreign-language phrase books. These books give all the phrases you will ever want, but with no way of finding them, at least not under the stress in which these phrases are generally needed—at midnight, perhaps, on a ferry dock, trying to look for a phrase like "I left my blue bag at the hotel," with a frenzied Italian porter pressing five fingers to his forehead, and yanking them away as if trying to pull out his brains and shouting *"Lire! Lire! Lire!"* Things are no better with foreign-word dictionaries, which make finding the word you want easy, without helping you find what to do with it. There's no trick in looking up, say, "bag" in an English-French dictionary. It's fitting this into a sentence, like "I want a bag." "I had a bag." "I dream about bags." Or "I can't stand bags"—complete, cohesive, round little thoughts with direction and some velocity. Which leaves people in those strange predicaments in which everyone shouts "bag" triumphantly without being able to find a handle on the conversation.

In other words, dictionaries and phrase books express everything clearly except what you're trying to say, and they don't dispose of those little time bombs of word endings that make distinctions between things like "you're disgusted" and "you're disgusting." They rarely give useful guides to pronunciation, which means that in the rare event that a tourist finds what he wants to say, they do nothing to make it possible for him to say it so that a native realizes that he found it, as the tourist plods along from word to word, as if digging post holes. I know the French phrase, letter perfect, for "A drink of water, please," but I've never yet made a Frenchman, and much less a Frenchwoman, understand what I mean by it. Once I asked a woman who ran a small hotel, and whom I got to know, to tell me what I was doing wrong. She cocked her head attentively and told me to go ahead and say it, and when I was through she said, "They aren't trying, monsieur." But she was a very polite woman and was fond of me because I always turned the lights off in my room when I went out.

Another thing, people tend to look at tourists a bit unhappily when they refer to these language devices as if they were computing currency; the natives seem to feel that the sight of someone referring to a book and frowning and looking a bit puzzled when all he has to do is speak in a civilized language, is mildly insulting. They don't seem to feel this way about someone who just sits there looking helpless; it makes them feel needed and helpful, and the dictionary-user misses a lot of those warm little scenes in restaurants with six people, including the waiter, joyously engaged in trying to think of the English word for, say, "veal," discussing it with one another, holding consultations. Students join in the game. Students' girl friends take a try at it. Women sitting six tables away smile thoughtfully into space, trying to think of the word. The waiter starts doing charades up and down the aisle, puts his fingers to his head for horns, runs around in a little circle saying "moo." Aha! Great mutual congratulations.

The fact is that nothing short of learning a language properly works, and this is a tough job even for serious scholars. I have nothing but the greatest admiration for anyone who learns a second language. For one thing, speaking anything but your native tongue is a handicap that never ends. I knew a vivacious, cultured little Russian woman who learned to speak English well enough not only to carry on ordinary conversation with great animation but to write poetry in it. Yet after thirty-five years of this magnificent accomplishment she was still calling photographs "snop shats," ruining every sentence that had led up to it, and quite a few that followed. Most people who turn up to enroll in adult night classes to learn French and Spanish and German on the first frosty week in October, drop out by November, with lame excuses about children being sick or husbands dying. The reason is that they never really wanted to learn another language; they just fell in love with the idea of going back to school and recapturing their lost youth.

I can remember some adult French classes I've gone to. The students were so fascinating that I couldn't keep my mind on the course. I can remember the facial expressions of one plump, pleasant-looking middle-aged woman. As we students got to know one another during talks in the corridor, I learned that she had completed a twenty-five-year test of motherhood, bringing up three daughters who were always leaving home, and two rebellious sons, through the era of drugs, rock music and youth protests, not to mention one of those husbands who isn't quite sure how his shirts get laundered. I'd watch her as she sat there enjoying her first nights off in twenty-five years, trying to take the French teacher, a young man just a year older than her oldest son, seriously, and trying to concentrate on things like "the pen" is feminine. She just sat there smiling happily through French vocabulary tests she was supposed to be worried about, and would have had the same expression through German or Spanish, or even calculus or nuclear physics, as long as she could just sit there resting her feet and not having to do the dishes.

Kids are the ones with the stamina and motivation to learn languages (or anything else). One memory of France that will remain clear to me is that of a boy waiter, a pink-faced, smiling lad who was determined to learn English, along with a lot of other things that would help him run his own hotel some day—folding napkins, setting tables, dusting sideboards, popping ahead of guests in dark stairways with lighted candles during strikes, watching what they ordered at the table so he could have as many things they wanted as possible waiting for them the next time they came in for a meal. He went at the English language barrier like a ball player shagging out grounders, batting words back at the guests until he got a homer, or at least a base hit, "beurre," "burter," "booter," "butter," he'd keep saying right into your face. He'd be at it bright and early in the morning and late at night.

Children are great teachers of languages. They're polite, patient, good-humored, with clear piping pronunciations, and they're utterly intrigued by a grown person who doesn't know the name for *anything*. They stare at you, their faces alive with the fun of the game. If I had to learn a foreign language fast I'd spend as much time as I could with kids. And I might try to find a waitress who used to serve my wife and me breakfast in a hotel in Athens, a big sloppy girl with bulging buttocks and buttons missing from her blouse who took it upon herself to teach us one word of Greek a day. Her method had the virtue of the limited objective. She'd just slop up in her loose wedges, plop a couple of glasses of water in front of us, spilling some of it, say, *"Nero xrio,"* and stand there till we repeated it properly. Then she'd take our order and slop off and yell at the chef. I remember every word she taught us.

But the people who can really short-cut speech are mothers and teen-age girls. I remember a smiling Swiss girl telling my wife and me something with friendly agitation—something she was apparently going to bring us before an early morning train departure. My wife somehow got across to her clearly, by a kind of telepathy, that anybody who looked that much like our daughters couldn't bring us anything we didn't want, both of them smiling at one another, and twenty minutes later the girl brought up a thermos of hot coffee and some sandwiches for a before-dawn breakfast, and my wife gave her a squeeze of approval, proving that for really important things you don't need language at all.

Kids, Car Sickness
and Miss Jane Welch's Flower Shelf

One day when I was feeling a bit let down because
what with the price of meat and all, I couldn't afford
to go anywhere, I was wandering around an airport
pretending I was going somewhere. I just drifted
around, absorbing the sound of screaming jets, honking
taxis and the familiar atmosphere of travel, the confusion and anxiety of being bullied, shoved, snubbed, of
feeling tacky and wrinkled. I got into a long, almost
wholly European line-up and once again experienced
that warm, friendly feeling of a knuckle pressing steadily between my shoulder blades, the sensation of life
and emotion just inches away. A young man with a
bedroll and an Indian headband in another line a few
feet away, turned around on a little anxious man behind him and said, suddenly sounding as if he wore a
bowler hat and vest, "*Would* you mind?" A man with
geometrical sideburns who had joined my line-up five
minutes after I got into it, moved up furtively beside
me as if looking for something on the floor, then eased
ahead of me, and finally was standing right in front of
me. He turned around, smiled agreeably, and said,
"You came later," but by then I was in such a mellow

mood, recalling shiny Mediterranean mornings and
the smell of olive oil and roast chestnuts that I felt
like Scrooge on Christmas morning, almost saying
aloud, "A splendid fellow! A most alert chap!" Besides,
I wasn't really going anywhere, and I just said, "I
know," and smiled back at him, leaving him staring at
me, not quite sure he'd heard right.

I went to the coffee shop and ran into that slender
grey-haired, soft-voiced, pink-faced English traveller
who weighs about 118 pounds and holds his own
quietly all over the world. He and his wife left their
bags on a seat and went away for something and a
big, fierce-looking, bald-headed man with shoulders
like hatch covers put their bags on the floor and sat
down. When the Englishman came back he cleared
his throat gently and said, "You're sitting in my seat."
The big guy gave an amused little laugh at the
sight of such a slender old gent confronting him, as if
considering just biting him gently to make him go
away. "You have my seat," the Englishman said, with
no change of tone. "Seat empty," the big guy said, but
doubt was creeping into his voice, and I knew it was
the beginning of the end. "I went to buy a book," the
Englishman said, not moving. The big man began to
crumble around the edges. Finally he got up and said
to the world at large, "It's not fair." It wasn't, either.
He was no match for the Englishman, whose wife came
back just then. "A man tried to take our seat," the
Englishman said, opening his book. His wife just went
on arranging some bundles without showing any surprise at the outcome. *"Did* he!" she said.

A woman sitting in one of a row of seats in a passengers' lounge behind me, was desperately trying to
stop her kids squabbling about who got the seat

next to hers. She started allowing them strictly timed spells. She'd check her watch to make sure that her six-year-old son didn't sit in the chair a second longer than his sister, who was standing in front of him staring at him, waiting for him to get off, while the boy looked straight ahead, completely absorbed in having his full turn, humming infuriatingly. He kept this up till his mother reached over and shook him, at which point he got down slowly, looking at his sister with loathing. A third youngster had a game of her own going, announcing to the world of travellers, "I have to go to the bathroom."

It all reminded me of the years when my wife and I travelled with the kids by car, train and boat. Children love to fight while travelling as much as they do when they're not travelling, or more. One woman I know used to drive to Florida with three kids in the back seat and a fly swatter beside her in the front seat. She used the fly swatter with a fast back-hand stroke, without taking her eyes off the road, to break up fights that started behind her.

Children also love to go to the bathroom, which is an adventure involving new sights and splashing water. They make announcements on this subject at crucial times, like when you're next in line to get a visa, or running to catch a train, or are almost through customs with an undeclared camera. You can't just ignore these announcements, for although you're pretty sure the kid doesn't mean it, you'd feel like a rotten dog if she did.

One thing to remember when travelling with kids is to *never be embarrassed*. A child may spill soup all over some gent who looks like an ambassador sitting next to you in a dining car, but he probably has kids of his own, and if they're grown up, secretly wishes he had them back. I've seen men with faces as cold as faro dealers melt with parental love when one of my little girls dropped a spoonful of ice cream on their laps. Children make a lot of friends for you when you're travelling. People like to pick them up and stand them on their feet when they fall. There's a new school of psychology that says you shouldn't do this, and some modern fathers will hold their hands out sternly, stopping all rescue efforts, while the little tyke struggles to her feet, but it spoils a lot of fun for old folks, who don't have much, and anyway kids like to be picked up.

Kids like to vomit, too; it's more fun than crayons, watching adults leap for bags and buckets. Children do a lot of this in cars—and Science doesn't know why. Doctor Alan Brown, who was physician-in-chief at the Hospital for Sick Children in Toronto, has suggested giving the child light, easily digested food before a car trip, but ends up by advising the parents to carry a thick plastic bag and a towel, or to see a doctor, and if none of these things worked, not to drive anywhere. Doctors Frances Ilg and Louise Bates Ames, authors of *Child Behavior,* have said that one theory of the cause of car sickness is that the child hates his mother. They hastened to add that they didn't believe this, and suggested that the mother might try singing to the child or putting a patch over one eye, as the child might be seeing too much.

Car sickness is a mysterious thing. A city nurse told me that she sometimes wondered if people plant the idea in a child's head by saying, "When you vomit, vomit in this bag," at which point the kid begins to look forward to a bit of action. It can be stopped the same way by the child's father saying loudly, "Daddy is attaching these straps to the car so you won't get car sick." Static straps, those straps you see dangling from bumpers, are supposed to drain static electricity from cars, and thus cure car sickness, usually in children, but sometimes in adults. A woman I once talked to about this told me that if her static straps are stolen she can tell right away because she starts to feel sick and get a headache. "I say to my husband, 'Somebody's stolen them straps.'" One man told me that he used to have static straps on his car but he had to take them off because they made him drowsy and he tended to doze off at the wheel. Static straps have won a mystical devotion equal to anything that's happened since people first began telling one another their moons were in Virgo. Perhaps in the near future we'll see them trailing behind jet-liners in an attempt to stop children getting air sick. But they'll still want to go to the bathroom whenever the "Fasten Seat Belts" sign goes on.

Right after the little girl in the airport had announced to me and everyone else who happened to be within earshot that she wanted to go to the bathroom, I had a coffee and spent an interesting twenty minutes playing an old game of mine, the game of trying to figure out the announcements made over the airport public address system by the grandsons and granddaughters of the men who used to announce train departures so nobody could understand them. As my coffee arrived a man gave a depressed sigh into the speaker system, put his head inside a barrel, cupped his hands over his mouth and announced, what sounded to me like: "Will Miss Jane Welch take her flower shelf off the eight ball. Thank you." Then he gave a kind of squawk, as if someone had stolen up behind him and garotted him.

I sat there staring into my coffee, pretty sure I hadn't heard right, but wondering what could have led up to this announcement if I *had* heard right. The most likely story seemed to me that this Jane Welch was a shy, unmarried elderly lady who lived in a village and had always wanted to travel, and had finally got the nerve up to take a trip to London. She'd closed up her house and arranged for a friend to look after her cat, but she had a fancy flower shelf that she knew her next-door neighbor would steal as soon as she left. So she decided to take it with her, carrying it to try to avoid paying excess luggage, which annoyed Air Canada, who kept badgering her every place she stopped for a rest. The minute she'd rest her flower shelf on something they would tell her to take it off. Somewhere in the airport was a poolroom, and Jane Welch had slipped in there pretending she was going to shoot a game of snooker, but really to rest her flower shelf on the pool table. The Air Canada announcer spotted her and announced, "Will Miss Jane Welch take the flower shelf off the eight ball."

I made notes on other announcements, with possible explanations.

"Gate Thirty-four. Gate Thirty-four. Sky caps. Shake hands please."

Two porters had been fighting over someone's luggage and had been seen from the control tower.

"Sky cap! Sky cap! Take a counter to Canadian Pacific."

A CP Air pilot, just before taking a flight out of Vancouver had been at a cocktail party given by an advertising agency to introduce a new brand of panty hose called "Count Your Blessings," and had been given a sales promotion novelty, a little metal abacus by a public relations man as he left. He had been working at it all the way to Toronto whenever the plane was on automatic pilot and had got so intrigued by it that when he lost it just as he was coming in for his landing, he told his radio operator to send a message to the terminal to get him another one. But the operator couldn't remember "abacus," and just said, "Take a counter to Canadian Pacific."

"Hi! Fillerup! At Gate Eight A."

This was some pilot who recognized a friend in the control tower as he was coming in for a landing, nearly out of gas.

"Go and fold it at Gate Fourteen."

A new folding airplane that had just arrived and the pilot didn't know what to do with it.

Sometimes all the announcers started to play tricks on one another.

"Oh, for . . . !" one announcer said, and shut off.

A girl kept saying, "Mr. Thelminoff! Mr. Thelminoff!" then added coyly, "Mr. Jolly may."

"Mr. Dana Superfort!"

"Capitol Allies stole this. Please report." And all this was happening at an airport in a country where I speak the language.

A Lot More Interesting
Than Taking Pictures

The other night I was at the home of a friend who every now and then would feel out the guests with little tentative remarks like "I don't suppose anyone wants to see our slides of Sweden?" He'd give a little laugh, playing it safe, as if he were only fooling, in case everyone said, "You're right." But you could see that he was ready to get out his 10,000 slides and unfold his screen if he got any encouragement at all. As soon as he'd say this, everyone else would smile and start to talk about something else, like how hard it was to find parking space these days, or turn to his daughter and ask her how she was doing at school. Everyone else, that is, except one grey-haired woman neighbor who sat in a corner not saying very much. Every time the idea of looking at slides of Sweden seemed to be safely dropped, this sadist would say, "Well, *I'd* like to see them." So it ended in that familiar scene, the man clicking the projector and saying, "That was our guide. Was he ever a character!" while I began trying to think up new remarks like "Your camera takes long distances very well, doesn't it?" and wondering how long it would take that round thing to make a complete circle. I also began to wonder why people don't go in for more original travel hobbies.

For instance, they could try to find relatives in the towns their grandparents came from or discover the origins of some of the ideas they grew up with and took for granted in North America. One example is the closed-up Sunday that I remember from my boyhood in Toronto, a city that in my youth was made up almost entirely of English, Irish and Scots people who preserved their old-country customs, like stiff and formal Sundays. As kids, we used to get through Sunday the best way we could. There were no movies or ball games. We weren't allowed to play on the street or to make any noise. We put on our best blue-serge suits, ate roast beef dinner at noon, and nearly went mad with boredom while our parents fell asleep under little tents made of the Sunday papers. There was no card playing on Sunday either, leaving little for even adults to do but go to church or sleep, or both. It was a day of completely suspended animation.

The Mediterranean siesta today comes close to this feeling, when you lie in bed in mid-afternoon feeling your nerves vibrate, but I came across the real origins when I went to the place my grandfather came from, a coal-mining town in the dead centre of England, a sombre little red brick community of 17,000. According to a brochure I'd read the town was recorded in a Norman survey of the year 1086 and before that was owned by a Saxon named Levenot, and the day I was there it gave the impression that nothing much had happened since he sold it, or gave it away. I began to realize where the Toronto Sundays of my boyhood originated.

I wandered around trying doors, but they were all locked. The Double Diamond was closed. The Pear Tree was closed. The Crown was closed. The Rose and Crown was closed. The Cock was closed. The fish and chips shop was closed. I had a vision of 17,000 people all snoozing quietly under the Sunday comics, and I decided to find out if any of them were my relatives. There was a phone booth on the square. I found two Allens in the book, spread out a pocketful of coins and called one of the numbers. A girl answered the phone and I pictured her delight at something breaking the Sunday coma, but her mother came to the phone and said she had an Aunt Dolly in Philadelphia but none of her family had emigrated to Canada. She said, "Cheerio," and presumably went back to sleep.

I tried the other Allen but got no answer. I wandered around wondering where to go next. Finally I met a useful fellow, the only other person in town besides a cold-looking cop and myself who was moving. He was letting himself into the town hall to do some work, and he took me inside to consult a voters' list. I left with the names of several Allens—Ethel Allen of Nottingham Road, Thomas Allen of Heague, Winifred Allen of Butterly Hill, Edgar Allen on Chappel Street, Cecil Edgward Allen on Greaves, Leonard Allen on Slack Lane, William Allen on Heathe Street, William James Allen on Argyle Road and one Allen, an example to the lot of us, who had risen to be the Right Reverend Geoffrey Allen, Parish Church of All Saints, Bishop of the Diocese of Derby.

I walked up dark brick alleys and opened little iron gates, knocked on the doors of red brick cottages and stood listening to the wind, looking over low red brick walls along empty streets. On my last call, a small man with wild hair standing on end came to the door of a red brick house and we both stared at one another. The wind was blowing and my own hair was now standing on end in the wind. The man in the doorway and I both realized dimly that there was something strange about the scene. Then it struck us what it was. We looked alike.

But he said that he had no relatives living abroad and I turned to leave. "I'm Robert Allen," I said.

"I'm Thomas Allen," he said, beginning to close the door. Thomas is my middle name, and when I left I was convinced that I had plenty of relatives inside those red brick cottages, but they were all sound asleep.

It was raw, red-nosed weather and a waitress in the hotel I stayed at that night heard me sneeze; she came over and told me to take Beecham's powders in a little bit of water. Later a porter showed me into a room so cold I could see my breath. He bustled around and lit the gas grate, said it would take about an hour to warm up, pulled the drapes and said that would make it *look* warmer anyway, then, when I was out for supper trying to get warm, sneaked in and put two hot-water bottles in my bed. The waitress and the porter set me pondering whether it is better to be cold and cared for, or warm and forgotten—or are material or moral values the greater good? To debate these things while your nose sticks over the quilt as cold as a spaniel's, engaging in an imaginary dialogue about whether happiness is simply the absence of pain; (or to take a specific case, are you happier gradually warming up under an English comforter, after making a dash in your pyjamas across a cold room, than you would have been if you'd been warm all evening, as you would have in North America)—is as good as a lecture in philosophy, and a lot more interesting than taking pictures.

"What Kind of Bird Is That?"

One way the jaded tourist can revive his interest in sight-seeing is to turn his attention to nature, and, instead of observing castles and restaurants, start observing, say, birds, which show a lot more variety as one moves around the world than waiters and castles. The people of most countries have little to say about the subject. Once I asked a French cab driver, whom I'd hired to drive me through the country, "What kind of a bird is that?" He tapped the instrument panel of his Citroën and said, "Tough!"—after a moment I realized that he was talking about its texture in a stew.

The tourist industry by and large ignores birds, yet there are many birds that I, for one, would like to see more than a lot of the things I see advertised. Japan has a blue robin, and an azure-winged magpie, a species that oddly has one population in Japan and one in Spain, and none anywhere else. Israel, which tends more and more to stress tourist sights like blast furnaces, making a tour of the Holy Land sound like a visit to Gary, Indiana, has 400 species of birds, of which 100 are resident or casual visitors—the hoopoe; the white stork; a goldfinch with a red mask; a Palestine sunbird; a Dead Sea sparrow, which looks much like the English sparrow, *Passer domesticus* but is called *Passer moabiticus;* an owl, *Athene noctua,* which looks just like the one symbolizing the goddess Athena on Greek coins; and some interesting mammals, including a big Indian crested porcupine and an Etruscan shrew. In my opinion the sight of any of these would restore some of the excitement of travel that has been lost by modern tourists—as it had been lost by the nineteen-year-old girl described in a recent magazine article ("Caravans of youth converge on Athens, Amsterdam, Istanbul") who had been "sitting around smoking dope in Amsterdam," and decided suddenly it would be better "sitting around smoking dope at home with friends."

Long before Richard Bach turned seagulls into a million-dollar industry, I'd spent many delightful, useless hours watching gulls, particularly the way they land. Somehow the sight takes me back to my boyhood, when I used to have a dream in which I'd take a run and jump over the clothes-line fences around the front lawns of the street where I grew up. When I started to come down, I'd just pull my feet up a bit and coast a little further, so that by a process of infinite division I would never land, although I'd be gliding along closer to the ground, amazing my friends and a woman named Mrs. Elliott who was always chasing me off her lawn. I'd glide past, almost touching her lawn but not quite, tipping my cap to her.

Gulls come in like this, close to the sand, banking, side-slipping, adjusting wing angles, their yellow legs pulled up close to their bellies, looking as if they could coast forever. Then they drop their landing gear, touch down, take three or four quick steps, give a little ruffle of their wings and hitch their shoulders to settle the feathers, like a man trying on a new jacket in front of a mirror; then they face into the wind, half close their eyes and look at you slyly.

Unlike sea hawks, who beat laboriously up and down the shore hunting for fish, looking earnest and industrious, as if studying for degrees in business administration, the gulls give the impression of loafing around a poolroom with their hands in their pockets.

One of the group is always taking off on some little excursion, and coming back. It always reminds me of the way on my street one of the gang would look around, as if sampling the air, say, "I'm going downtown," and leave. A while later he'd come back with a mysterious look, saying nothing about what he did, or saw, but implying that he'd met four or five agreeable girls down there. If the guy had a car, he came back to a fancy stop in front of the waiting gang, doing some precision steering. The returning gull does the same, sliding past the other gulls about six inches off the sand, separated from everything earthbound by about six inches of air, looking secretive and as if thinking of something.

The gulls always seem to be waiting around for something to happen, the way we used to. If you toss a piece of bread in the air, they come from other parts of the beach, hardly visible at first, flying low over the sand, until there are thirty or forty or more in a wild, hilarious game like one we used to call "Hog." They make fast sweeping runs downwind past you, wheel and turn back into the wind and come to a stop in midair, a splash of pure white against a deep blue sky, looking at the piece of bread out of round, gold-colored eyes, in which you can see the black pupils, which have a fierce, fiendish hypnotic stare. Occasionally they have midair collisions, with a dry brushing sound, and a fight breaks out sometimes when one lands too close to another. A gull will charge, hump its back, lower its head and scream and curse and make stretching motions with its neck, and give that seagull cry that sounds of the sea. They put on magnificent flying exhibitions and great chases, one trying to get a piece of bread from another in midair, swooping over the dunes, zooming up, wheeling, doubling back. Once I watched a gull chase a plover that got in on the game; it kept right on the plover's tail, like a DC-8 tagging a World War I Sopwith Camel.

One familiar gull that goes south with the tourists in North America is the ring-billed gull, a bird with a soft-blue back and polka-dot wing tips that you see in the plowed fields and on summer cottage docks in the North in summer. Ring-billed gulls winter as far south as Mexico, and in cold windy weather, when the sand streams across the beach in ribbons and the tops of the waves are smoking, the gulls stand facing north with their shoulders hunched and their eyes closed, their legs in sudsy water. Or they hang still in the air, as if dangling from invisible wires, or glide downwind, wings motionless, their bodies wriggling like fish.

In fine weather they stand on the wet sand, each gull joined by two thin legs to its reflection hanging upside down with another sky below it. Sometimes a gull stands on one leg, head twisted around, beak buried in its feathers, dozing, but if you come within fifteen feet its head comes around and the other foot comes down and it eases oceanward, head turned sideways so it can keep an eye on you.

They sometimes spend ten minutes or so digging their beaks into their backs and chests, giving themselves a good shaking, like feather dusters, scratching their jaws, dabbling their beaks in the water, peering down as if they heard something ticking—in fact, not doing much of anything.

Bird watching for the traveller doesn't necessarily involve bird books and binoculars. One of the important things to do in Lucerne, for instance, is to feed the water birds, a fine, lazy way to spend a couple of hours in a warm sunny afternoon in September. You buy a franc's worth of dried corn kernels, drape yourself over the railing, and toss them one by one into the water, or in handfuls, and watch the breakdown of the bird community. The male swans peck the females, bully them and chase them away; the females prang the ducks; the male ducks chase the female ducks; the female ducks tug feathers out of the coots, if they don't give up their rights. The female coots are the lowest on the bulling scale, but they're small, fast and determined and get most of the food, darting around, diving, running over the water like little motor boats, looking eager, undignified and ambitious. It's a nice thought to take with you when you go back to your hotel, thinking of how you're going to have to hustle when you get home to pay for your trip to Switzerland.

Hotel Conventions—
An Interesting Phenomenon

One of the tricks of travel today is learning how to
deal with the hotel convention, an American idea that
has spread to Europe, where you often have trouble
getting a room because a convention of 3,500 police-
men arrived there ahead of you, or 3,500 chemists, or
florists.

The convention is a big thing in the travel industry
now. I was in a Four Seasons-Sheraton a while ago
in which amid the coffee shops, bars, lounges and ball-
rooms there were fourteen meeting rooms, and an ex-
hibition hall that trucks could drive into (they do,
too, to unload displays of merchandise for conventions). Holiday Inns, who love conventions, are spread-
ing the idea right to Kyoto, Japan, and Singapore, and
soon, probably, you'll be able to look up at Mount
Everest while listening to visiting members of, say, the
Optimists Club all roaring with laughter before breakfast (a sound I heard once in Fresno, California, and
haven't quite forgotten), or you'll be privileged to sit
in the Blue Room of the Hilton Taj Mahal experiencing
that moment in the banquet-room when there's a sudden hush, the last waiters close the doors, there's the

rumble of well-fed men of affairs shoving their chairs
back from tables, and a thin, nervous man gets up and
says: "As I came here today I was reminded of the
story about the librarian who sat on a camera . . ."

Some of these conventions must be a real cultural
shock to the natives. The other day I talked to a man
I've known for years who had just come back from a
life insurance convention in Fiji. It was strange to listen
to this man, who, for forty-five years, from stripling
office boy to vice-president of group sales, had looked
at nothing more exotic than a glass partition with little
printed messages pasted on them, like "LUCK IS PLUCK
plus PERSEVERANCE," as he told me about his trip, standing there in his tenth-story office, his cheeks a bit pink
and puffy, looking out at the murky late afternoon traffic. As he talked, I started to form images of insurance
salesmen singing "For He's a Jolly Good Fellow" to the
Top Ten Salesmen, while within a couple of spear
throws were Irene the Hula Dancer and plump Fijian
prostitutes, and without in the languid, warm night
were Fijians chuckling about their ancestors' habits of
eating one another.

Many conventions, nevertheless, are of interest in
themselves, and the thing to do about them is not to
grumble about the shortage of rooms, or about some
tourist attraction like the re-enactment of the visit of
Hamlet's father being sold out for a week, but to join
the convention, which is apt to be a more interesting
experience than a visit to Elsinore. The last convention
I mingled with was an anthropologists' convention. I
was particularly interested because although anthropologists have published some fascinating papers on
things like growing up in Samoa, nobody has published a paper on growing up among anthropologists,

something I know a bit about myself, having two anthropologists in the family. As an anthropologist might put it, the following brief study is based on notes I made during five hours of non-participant research conducted in rooms, corridors and coffee shops.

Among their many skills, anthropologists produce round, well-shaped sentences with apparently no effort. One tall, bearded anthropologist in yellow buckskin boots said, as he passed me in the hall, "I don't think we should cast ourselves in the role of watchdogs for justice," a sentence that would have taken me half an hour amid smouldering cigarette butts to come up with. They also use a lot of sign language: for instance, they often make little circular motions with their index fingers in front of their chins when explaining something, as if winding up fishing lines. And they have very analytical minds. One man, talking about his dog back home in Illinois, said, "Shermen is a hundred and twenty pounds of beast and people say he's stupid, but I don't think he's stupid at all, I think he's smart enough to play it cool."

Anthropologists, particularly the young, are very neat about their surroundings. In one room during a symposium on Indian land loss in Virginia, a woman named Helen C. Rountree said, "I'm going to drone at you for about five minutes, then you can fire away at me." I had just noticed two empty C-Plus tins and two Canada Dry tins lying on the rug along with a crumpled drinking straw, when two young anthropologists came by. A male and a female—and apparently from different tribes as they showed no recognition of one another—they bent over quickly, picked up the tins and the straw, put them in a wastepaper basket, and sat down cross-legged on the floor. This was not a form of attention getting, like the ceremonial ecology chants of oil company men.

Anthropologists dress in bush jackets, jeans, slacks, running shoes, snow boots, Nehru coats, ponchos and buckskin breeches. Most males have beards, and both sexes often sit cross-legged on the floor smoking little clay pipes. Members are very much aware of food and lodging. One mature female with grey hair tied in a ponytail, who told me she lectures on medical anthropology in Kentucky, looked sideways at me while eating a hamburger in the coffee shop, swallowed, and said she'd never found better food or service anywhere in the world and she hoped the association chose this place next year for its convention. A tall male who overheard her leaned over a small female anthropologist wearing Indian beads, and said, "It's a manifestation of the national culture."

Anthropologists tend to be quiet, and rarely cheer or slap one another on the back. I was at a convention on the day before a big football game and a non-anthropologist from some far-off region arrived at the hotel carrying a suitcase and shouting, *"Yay! Rough-riders!"* The anthropologists stood in dignified, reserved little groups looking at him in complete silence. The stranger, exhibiting the interesting universal custom of saving face, kept on smiling as if nothing had happened, but he soon disappeared into the dense, protective undergrowth of a nearby bar.

I wasn't able to find any published source material for my study of anthropologists, but I talked to one person who had been watching them for five days, a coat-check woman with the unmistakable features and speech of a small, threatened group, the Wasps. When I asked her how anthropologists compared with people at other conventions, she said, "Gees, they're like a bunch of hippies. They're nice, though, and they're quiet. They don't drink much. We had twenty-five television people in here yesterday and they made more noise than all the anthropologists put together. A lot of them are broke. They just slept on the floor last night. Are they intelligent, though!" She leaned on her counter and looked down the corridor where in her day she has seen many strange customs, and said thoughtfully, "They're nice-looking young people. Even those guys with the beards and long hair are good-looking young fellows."

Some rituals of the anthropologist aren't what they appear to an outsider. There were about 850 talks and film showings at the convention, with titles like "Some Observations on Social Mobility in Early Historic Indo-European Societies," but anthropologists don't come to hear the talks, which are just an excuse to have the convention. What they come for is to meet other anthropologists, find out about where to get jobs, and where to get papers published. Wandering along the corridors, you hear a lot of talk about papers. "Once I get my paper copied," I heard one man say, "I don't have to freak out about losing the original."

In conclusion, I must state that I found that anthropologists form one of the healthiest, most cheerful, intelligent, friendly tribes I've studied in a long time, and if their number keeps increasing, as it has in recent years, I can't think of a better thing that could happen to mankind. If you must stay at a hotel with lots of conventions, choose an anthropologists' convention if you can.

"Expecting Ease Everywhere
But Where I Am"

Travel has changed drastically since it began in the 1700's with rich young Englishmen and Germans taking the Grand Tour, often financed by their families who wanted to get rid of them. The Grand Tour was a three-year trip by coach or horseback, with a tutor, to France, Italy and the Low Countries, with the traveller sometimes being carried, bodily, by porters, over the mountain passes, into Italy. Doctor Johnson, the eighteenth-century English essayist, a traveller himself, said that it was the best thing for a youth when he started "running after women and bad company."

There had been travel for ages before this. In A.D. 173 Pausanias wrote ten books on his tour of Greece, describing things like the Acropolis, and the Theatre of Athens, which was around 600 years old then. But travellers were rare, and very rich and travelled with an entourage of a hundred or so slaves, their own furniture, cooks, musicians and guards.

Gibbon wrote that Theodora, the Byzantine empress, when advised by her physicians to use the Pythian warm baths, took along on her trip the Praetorian praefect, the great treasurer, several counts and patricians, and a train of four thousand attendants.

The guards were not just for show. Travel wasn't safe, then or later. In medieval times, hotel guests slept with their knives on their chests, and some innkeepers made a nice living out of murdering and robbing their clients. There was always the risk, too, of robbers riding out of the woods on the lone traveller. Safety was one of the reasons why Chaucer's pilgrims banded together on the way to Canterbury, and in Chaucer's time there was danger from pirates or privateers when crossing the English Channel. As late as 1774 travel was still a risky business in England. Writing of travel in England, Horace Walpole complained that roads were so infested with highwaymen, that it was dangerous to travel even by day.

Even the richest traveller taking the Grand Tour abroad often had to put up with rough treatment. Tourists were hated everywhere, just as English labourers often hooted at foreigners, and English travellers spoke to no one but Englishmen and sometimes not to them. Smollett told of an Englishman who had travelled for three days in France with two other Englishmen without speaking to either of them and Hazlitt reported exchanging only two sentences with a fellow Englishman with whom he travelled in France. Halfway to their destination Hazlitt's fellow traveller asked, "How far is it to Evreux?" Hazlitt said, "I don't know" and that was it.

Foreigners were considered funny. James De Mille, a Canadian who was well travelled and wrote a series of articles on Europe called *The Dodge Club Stories,* a forerunner of Mark Twain's *Innocents Abroad,* used people of foreign lands as comical props, and had his characters shout things like "washy, washy," at Italian landladies when they wanted their laundry done.

It's interesting that even in those days the travel syndrome was appearing. Goldsmith wrote to a friend on August 2, 1758, from Poland, "When will my wanderings be at an end? When will my restless disposition give me leave to enjoy the present hour? When at Lyons, I thought all happiness lay behind the Alps; when in Italy, I found myself still in want of something, and expected to leave solitude behind me by going into Romelia; and now you find me turning back, still expecting ease everywhere but where I am. It is now seven years since I saw the face of a single creature who cared a farthing whether I was dead or alive. Secluded from all the comforts of confidence, friendship, or society, I feel the solitude of an hermit, but not his ease."

Some of the scenes in Dickens' *Little Dorrit* give a pretty accurate picture of a traveller today coming apart with nerves and wounded ego.

> "Is it possible, sir," said Mr. Dorrit, reddening excessively, "that you have—ha—had the audacity to place one of my rooms at the disposition of any other person? . . . . I will not occupy any salon. I will leave your house without eating or drinking, or setting foot in it. How do you dare to act like this? Who am I that you—ha—separate me from other gentlemen?"

Mass travel began in the 1800's with Cook's tours, and the wealthy were horrified by it. One novelist, Charles Lever, wrote about the "awful specimens of men and women to be found abroad," and accused

Cook of reducing the traveller to the level of "these creatures."

Following the last world war travel has become so widespread that today's restless tourist is in constant search of new places to see. "People come in here," one travel agent told me, "you wouldn't think they had the nerve to go downtown. They buy tickets around the world. I had a woman in yesterday who was going around the world. We routed her through Bangkok. I mentioned that for another two hundred dollars she could go home by way of Sydney, Australia, and she took that too."

One result of people searching so frantically for novel places is that they overlook the joy of going back to familiar places. One of the reasons I keep going back to Florida, for instance, is pure nostalgia.

My wife and I have rented the same place there, on and off, for twenty years, and have left odds and ends of our things there. This year when we wanted to make a cup of coffee before the gas had been turned on, my wife went right to a cupboard beneath the kitchen sink and produced a hotplate, a bit rusty, that we had bought in 1954, when we first drove to Florida. We used it just once, in a place outside New York called Brown's Cabins, where my wife daintily draped the only surface near an electric plug, the toilet seat, with a pink towel, and we made toast and warmed up some soup for the kids, then abandoned forever the idea of cooking on the road.

I'm surrounded by familiar things—a desk lamp in the shape of a gilded Buddha, a $3.50 bookcase, half a set of the eleventh edition of the Encyclopaedia Britannica, a broom I broke four years ago and glued together and bound with a wet rope so that, when it dried, it was like a sleeve of steel; two clothes-line posts of cypress that I put up eighteen years ago, and a piece of linoleum I tacked to some planks so my wife wouldn't get sandspurs in her toes when she hung out the washing; two nails I arranged in the front porch and painted with my wife's pink nail polish that indicate true north, which I worked out from the stars; even a weed that each year grows four feet above my veranda floor through a crack between sprung planks. Last year when my landlady visited me, she pulled it up before I could catch her, and it took a couple of weeks before it grew up again and waved at me gracefully in the ocean breeze.

I like the feeling of continuity about the place, which was built, but never finished, by a ship's carpenter, and the sense of succeeding generations. Sometimes I see, sitting staring at me from the scrub like old memories, descendants of my kids' cat, a wild, fertile, ferocious beast called Tabby, who used to leap up into the front stubs of the cabbage palms like a bad dream. But my kids loved him and used to hug him and kiss him while he looked balefully out from their arms watching for dogs, which, if they were under a foot and a half high, he could lick. He could, and did, lick all cats, usually in full, terrifying view, on a sandy patch I keep clear with a scythe outside my back door among the stinging nettles, cactus, sandspurs, sea oats, dune grass, palmetto scrub and yucca.

I like my landlady, a gentle woman from Brooklyn who does little things to lure me back each year, like giving a coat of aluminum-colored Derusto to the gas pipe railing beside the steps that amble up the dune to my cottage. These steps start as a piece of sagging plywood, become more progressive for a few levels as

concrete blocks, then arrive on top as a piece of an old
hatch cover. But the main thing is, they lead to a place
where I can disappear from view. I can get through
the winter there with a pair of pants I bought at a place
called Syd's for $10.95, three sports shirts I bought
for $1.89 each at the Publix supermarket, and a pair
of running shoes just right for one of my spare-time
pursuits, salvaging lost kites that people buy for their
kids on their way south but don't know how to fly. I
find them speared on my Spanish bayonets, with strings
trailing out over a gully between my place and the
sea where the growth is as thick as a bird's nest, and
where nobody will go except me. I've found some dandies down there, with fancy dragon's tails, that would
set you back two or three dollars.

Occasionally people who have been reading about
new life-styles in the sun come to the door and ask if
they can see through the cottage, which they think
they might like to buy; but they don't stay very long.
A while ago I showed a nervous-looking woman and
her daughter around. The woman kept looking uneasily
out my south window at a densely covered dune from
which came occasional fluttering and scurrying sounds,
and where palmettos blowing in a rising ocean wind,
kept tapping the windows with long fingers. The older
woman was asking if we ever saw snakes in there when
a lizard I know that lives under my back porch got in
the back door. I started chasing it around our old Duo
Therm heater with an up-ended wastepaper basket,
and the next we heard from the woman was a polite
little note saying, "Your cottage is darling. Thank you
for letting us see it, but mother has decided to go back
to Pittsburgh." What she really had decided, of course,
was to look for the Florida she'd been reading about—

which has nothing to do with my Florida, just as the Europe Oliver Goldsmith had read and heard about turned out to have nothing to do with the Europe he visited "still expecting ease everywhere but where I am."

28

Looking at
Government Buildings—Inside

Now that the average tourist has seen the main government buildings of the Western world—the Capitol in Washington, for instance, and Parliament Buildings in London—and is wondering what else to look at, he can do it all over again—watching what goes on *inside* the buildings and discovering what governments actually do when they're at work.

I've always pictured a session of Parliament as a scene of fiery oratory and dramatics like, say, a scene from *The Winslow Boy*, with Robert Donat, but it isn't like that at all. At least it wasn't the day I was in Ottawa. There were only about a dozen Members scattered around the 264 seats, and the feeling in the old chamber, with its rows of bright-green blotters, gold-leaf cornices, carved white oak desk fronts and hand-painted Irish linen ceiling, was kind of cosy and restful, like a rainy day at the cottage. The inaudibility of the speeches had the relaxing effect of raindrops, with somebody over in the New Democratic corner talking about fertilizer and nobody listening to him, except perhaps Mr. Speaker, who sat in a chair like a throne, rubbing his hands over his forehead as if he had a slight headache.

During each speech the other Members read newspapers, got up and disappeared through curtains at sides of the room, like people going into tents, came back and sat down, maybe jeering at the man giving the speech. When a Member of Parliament makes a joke, he immediately turns to a deskmate and they both laugh, as if he'd just thrown a spitball at the teacher. One man said something about a hound out in his part of the country that sat on a cactus and was too lazy to get up. Everyone on his side thumped their desks. But the man went on, it was all the same: sitting, standing or lying down. A Liberal called out something about trying standing on his head, I think. His side laughed and slapped their desks.

Speakers looked hurt and indignant. Men shouted to get to the point. When one man stood up, a Member in a pink shirt said: "Here comes the end of the parade," and walked out. Once during some puzzling exchange, a Member called across the green rug, "Where have *you* been all afternoon? *You* were sitting there." "I've been working." "Shame!" A man gave his pants a hitch and said he wasn't ashamed to be a Canadian. Another man said something about betrayal of our nation and gave *his* pants a hitch.

The Progressive Conservatives just kept reading newspapers or talking to one another. One man sat clutching the back of his head with splayed fingers. Another looked into space, twirling a chain. Somebody said the Leader of the Opposition had been shedding crocodile tears, and another man gave a talk I couldn't hear about a schoolgirl trying to learn French. One man during his speech said, "You could almost be

biblical and say, 'Ye shall not live by bread alone,'"
and somebody laughed. Six Liberals, four Progressive Conservatives and two New Democrats talked right
through a speech by Grace MacInnis (NDP, Vancouver Kingsway) in which she said we could all wash
something down with Coca-Cola and if the government
kept on with some policy we might as well send
Canada floating down the Mississippi, while the Minister of Trade and Commerce looked across the room at
someone I couldn't see and gave an okay sign with
thumb and finger.

Mr. Speaker told one man to confine his remarks to a
bill, while the Member took a sip of water and sat
there looking chastened. Everyone on the opposite side
looked pleased. Mr. Speaker said something in a tiny
voice and all the NDP's shouted *"Yea!"* He said
something else in a tiny voice and all the Liberals
shouted *"Nay!"* A young guy beside me said, "It's
better than TV."

But it was kind of nice in there. You found yourself
picturing a girl out in Nanaimo bent over her books
studying French and farmers counting bags of fertilizer, and the headwaters of the Mississippi, and an
old hound backing into a cactus out in south Saskatchewan: and it was nice knowing that somebody cared
about them. You can go into Parliament any day and sit
in the visitors' gallery, but you can't make notes, smoke
or take pictures.

You can take guided tours of the Parliament Buildings, under the watchful eyes of burly, big-chested
guards. The highlight of the tour is the library, a rich
old room of warm wood and wrought iron and towering
walls containing 250,000 volumes, with light globes
and gold bowls humbly presented by the goldsmiths of

England, and a huge white statue of Queen Victoria in the middle. In the crimson and gold Senate chamber the guide tells you that the chandeliers are held up by red tape. "The jokes come with the building," one guide told me later.

The guides are all university students and their favorite tourists are senior citizens who take a real interest in things. Elderly women pat the guides' cheeks when the tour is over and ask them where the washroom is. But all guides loathe Grade 7 and 8 schoolkids from Montreal and Toronto, who ask how much they're making and where they bought their suits and how much everything in the Parliament Buildings cost.

I stood under the inscription "The wholesome sea is at her gates, her gates both east and west," and asked a few visitors how they liked Canada's Parliament Buildings. A middle-aged man from North Carolina said he thought it was mighty pretty, and a young fellow from Cleveland in tattered blue jeans, with a girl in red stockings, said, "There may be more beautiful buildings in the world, but I've never seen them."

I went back into the House of Commons and stayed till late at night. The room was quiet and churchly. There were only three Members left, then only two. One got up and read a letter in a faint, faraway voice. The other man shouted, "False!" Somebody carried the mace down the aisle. A guard, who had been putting up seats, turned to me and said, "Finis," and I went out and listened to the nighthawks over Parliament Hill.

29

"Why Not Move to a Place Like This?"

One by-product of mass travel is that a great number of people, exposed to new scenes and ways of life, get the idea of moving, more or less permanently, to another country. These notions are often based on impulse, rising from various fleeting states of euphoria. A New York advertising man, say, takes a three-week vacation from the bedlam of trucks, taxis, concrete mixers and the rage of bus drivers being driven mad like everyone else by overpopulation. Perhaps he goes to Lucerne, and one day folds his coat up neatly, puts it on the planks behind him, loosens his tie, leans back ecstatically on the oars and skims out from shore on a sunny lake and a gentle wave of nostalgia, recalling boyhood scenes of catching catfish, getting sunburned, smelling of worms, fish, cucumber sandwiches, mud and bulrushes.

He says to himself, "By gosh! I've forgotten how to live! Why not *move* to a place like this?"—an inspiring thought, strengthened, later, when he leans over the fence of a Swiss farm exchanging greetings with a grey-brown bullock not much bigger than a bed toy, shoving his fist against its head, and feeling its pleasure coming right up through his arm. He sees a cat cross a sunny patch of barnyard thoughtfully, concentrating on something, like the meaning of life. He says to himself, "This is how civilization started," thinking with horror of meetings back in New York about how to break down consumer resistance to a new brand of toothpaste.

Or perhaps the guy is sitting at a sidewalk table in Paris, looking out at a street that looks as if it's cut from pastel-colored cardboard and as if it would sway gracefully if you leaned on it, pulling the treetops with it—dozing in the morning sun, a bit tight on wine, thinking, "This is the way to live!" (momentarily forgetting that he's on holiday, a good way to live anywhere, and that millions of Frenchmen are at work).

But the city or town or the country have nothing to do with it essentially. The thought may come to a housewife from Sheepshank, Wyoming, seeing New York for the first time, with all those shops; or to a motorist from Huntsville, Ontario, who is still wearing his snow boots, seeing the southern United States for the first time, watching cotton drift across a drowsy road. The point is, it's a new, exciting, pleasant and desirable condition, and there seems no logical reason for ending it: i.e., going home.

But although the world is shrinking in terms of flying time, and just about every country wants tourists, or, more accurately, their money, almost no country wants them to stay. All you need do is stand in an immigration office and listen to those questions: "Where is she now? Whose brother is he? Is it your sister's husband? Where is your brother-in-law now? Is he in Hungary?"

I heard one girl in a Canadian immigration department tell a man from Nigeria, "I cannot make exceptions. If you are studying here you are not living here." She pursed her lips, and, with an expression of counting to ten to keep her temper, looked out over a line of bewildered, anxious people clutching passports and fishing documents out of big homespun handbags. Not that Canada is any more hostile to newcomers than any other country. I've had American immigration men shout at me that they pay taxes to keep up highways, glaring at me as if I didn't; and in France I've had immigration girls look at me as if they thought all Canadians lived in tepees and should stay there.

Many people who want to emigrate to another country are motivated by a romantic idea that has been with man for many centuries, that of getting back to the simple life, in the northern bush, say, or on a South Sea island. This is something familiar to the provincial governments in Canada, who sell or lease crown lands (whether the applicant is a Canadian or not) on the lakes that lace the hard-rock forests of Quebec, Ontario, Manitoba and Northern Saskatchewan, and in other wild parts of the country. They're happy to do this, but these properties are for people who just want to live on the land, not *off* the land, all year, an idea that is quickly discouraged. The Canadian bush is no place for amateurs, particularly when the temperature drops down to a point at which hammering a nail into a two-by-four outdoors is a painful experience, like trying to drive it into steel, and dropping the hammer involves a little exercise in survival trying to find it again. It can be just as bad in summer, when the bush swarms with black flies, insects which caused one early Jesuit father, working his way by canoe along the French River, to comment that they put him through the worst martyrdom he'd yet experienced. During the Depression years in the 1930's, Canadian crown lands were given to the unemployed, free, for farming, but within a few years, fourteen out of fifteen farms were abandoned.

In Fiji, the government, faced with the problem of tourists who have always wanted to escape to a tropical island, makes them show a return ticket, and hands out a pamphlet explaining to visitors that if they move onto a tropical island around there they'll find they're trespassing on somebody's property.

Anyway, life isn't made up of emotional and aesthetic peaks. It's made up of the wide, dull plains in between. And under a hard topsoil of practical considerations, like immigration departments, visas, matters of citizenship, work permits, withholding taxes, residence status, most of us have a soft subsoil of personal background and loyalties where we have our roots.

Changing citizenship is generally an irrevocable step. The new naturalized citizen can never again be a native-born citizen of the country he was born and raised in, and if he wants to go back (as many do), has to wait, sometimes for years, to be allowed the rights he was born with, and then he never quite gets them all back again. He can be deported from his native land. Besides, it's often more of an emotional occasion than the applicant imagines it will be. Sometimes blasé world citizens cry at the crucial moment. Judges tend to be understanding and sympathetic. "I've seen a judge cry," one American lawyer told me. "We don't ask people to forsake their memories, you know," he said, sounding hurt that anyone would think this of him. "Just their allegiance."

I attended the naturalization ceremonies in a small town in the southern states one time when nine people were becoming Americans (although sometimes citizens are sworn in by the hundreds). I climbed the spiral staircase of an old cream-colored brick county courthouse. A small group of spectators sat in a worn-looking circuit courtroom, with two potted plastic palms, some vases of cut flowers, and a feeling of church. Nine people who had applied for citizenship sat on a bench including an Argentinian youth, a chunky, confused-looking grey-haired man from Austria, who had been in the United States since 1912, a tall, bony man from Jamaica, a girl from India, and a girl from France. One of the group was a Canadian, a trim middle-aged woman in a blue blouse with curly grey-blond hair and dark-rimmed glasses, who had been born in Hampshire, England. She had become a Canadian, she told me, turning and talking to me over a low partition, and she loved Canada, but she had been in the United States now for twelve years and felt it her duty to become a citizen of the country where she was making a living.

A pastor of the First Baptist Church in bright blue pants shook hands with the nine people, saying, "Welcome to this country," said Austria was a wonderful place, and that he'd been in Jamaica himself a week ago, asked the Canadian woman how things were up in Ottawa, spoke French to the French girl, and said, "Come visit us at the Baptist Church." Then we were told that we were all to show proper courtesy and decorum and to stand up when the judge arrived. The judge came in wearing his black robes, a youngish man with alert black eyes, greying sideburns and a

pleasant face that looked as if it were made of soft
rubber.

A short, plump, energetic lawyer said if it pleased
the court there were nine petitioners and each had
been found to be of good moral character. The judge
looked at him thoughtfully and put his finger on the
point of his nose and shoved it in flat, holding his
glasses in his teeth. A tall, grey-haired clerk of the
circuit court told everyone to raise his right hand and
repeat:

> I hereby declare, on oath . . . that I ab-
> solutely and entirely renounce and abjure . . .
> all allegiance and fidelity . . . to any foreign
> prince . . . potentate . . . state or sovereignty
> . . . of whom or which . . . I have heretofore
> been a subject or citizen. . . .

A truck passing outside the courthouse drowned out
some of their words. After "So help me God," there was
a prayer about defending, dying and protecting. Everyone seemed dry-eyed. A Legionnaire distributed a
booklet on how to fly the U.S. flag and made a short
speech. A member of the Civitan Club said, "Thank
you very much for becoming an American." A Daughter
of the American Revolution made a short speech. Another woman went along the row and pinned a lapel
pin of the flag to everybody. A woman from an organization called the Pilot Club distributed some little
potted plants so that each would have some U.S. soil.
The judge came down without his robes and shook
hands with everyone. Each was given a certificate.
People drifted off clutching their pamphlets and pres-
ents.

A middle-aged man came back and asked if a nat-

uralized American could become President, and the
lawyer said, "No, but there's always Vice-president,"
and left. Soon I was alone in the empty courtroom
looking at the judge's blotter, which needed replacing.
I heard someone in an office downstairs say, "How
many of these envelopes did you order, for Christ
sake!" I had a hot dog at the newsstand downstairs and
went into the basement washroom, where I read, over
the toilet, "The city council sits above us all," and over
the urinal, "Up the IRA."

I left. Out on the street one of the new citizens, a
handsome brown woman in a long dress, stood with
folded arms staring across the street at a Walgreen's
drugstore, looking as if in her thoughts she were standing under a banyan tree halfway around the globe.

I drove home along a beautiful old road and stopped
to look at some still woods and listen to a frog, and
thought of a woman I know who, all the time she swore
her allegiance to the United States, kept remembering
the lines she memorized as a schoolgirl, "whose heart
hath ne'er within him burned, as home his footsteps
he hath turned."

I stopped beside a sunny creek the color of strong
tea and watched three bright blue darning needles
dart over some yellow spiked water plants; I heard a
catbird that could have been in any other country,
down among some sunny weeds, giving his small rasp-
ing sound. I listened to the wind in the pines, which
sounded just like the wind in the pines in Norway or
Japan or Canada and I wondered how long it would
be before man stopped playing his pompous little games
of dividing up the earth and drawing borders and
swearing oaths, all of which seems, somehow, un-

real. The reality is something they take with them wherever they go.

The night of the day I saw the swearing-in ceremonies I visited a man who had moved his family to Florida, then started right in to organize a bagpipe band. This was practice night and the man, named McKay, said to the group that had gathered, "Okay, let's get out our pipes and see what happens." Awful sounds were already coming from outside, where a young lad named Will, who told me that his grandfather came from Dunfermline, was marching up and down in blue denims, striped polo shirt and running shoes, piping "Scotland the Brave" beneath a naked bulb in the carport. He strutted past power mower, brooms, mops, lawn chairs, a bicycle, brazier and shovels, with that controlled, delayed step used in pipers' parades, his manner as ceremonial as if he were outside Edinburgh Castle or Buckingham Palace, his white-fringed blue bag squeezed under his arm, red, white and blue ribbons flowing, the three drones going, chanter blaring. It's hard to believe so much racket can come from this one strange instrument.

Others came out and joined the fierce warlike wail. Mrs. McKay begin larruping her drum, twirling her clubs head bowed, studious and absorbed. A boy named Michael, who had taken a lot of kidding about the braces on his teeth, hitched his plaid pipes and joined the racket. McKay, tall and commanding, took his position at the front. The din was now approaching the sound level of a full-scale border raid. Looking out toward the back garden, where Spanish moss was lit up by a misty moon, you imagined you saw the heather blowing and men marching over the brow of a hill, kilts swaying. A smiling woman neighbor in a blue dress came over and stood there beaming, and was joined by a man with red sideburns and a soiled-looking little boy with no shirt and a halo of yellow hair, who had ridden over on a unicycle.

"Don't the neighbors complain?" I shouted at the man with red sideburns.

"They don't want to get involved," he hollered into my ear. *"They figure it's somebody being murdered."*

The noise was frightful. A dog barked. A passing motorist honked his horn. The little boy fell off his unicycle.

Through an open window I could see Lorne Greene on color TV, with nobody paying any attention to him, as the night was filled with the shrill, metallic, blaring music, partly awful, partly wonderful, wholly satisfying —a wild, sad, moving lament for the hills of home.

30

Canadians and Americans

One of the intriguing experiences of travel is that it gives you a different perspective on your own country-men when you see them away from home. When I was a kid I never questioned the going idea on my street that my fellow English-speaking Canadians repre-sented a sort of universal standard of behavior, and that Americans, for instance, were inclined to be loud, boastful and unstable, a conviction that lurked in the back of my head into adult life. But when I started com-ing across Canadians away from Canada, in the United States, I got a new impression, that Americans only appear noisy and gregarious when compared with Canadians, who, I realized, are cold, Nordic, reserved, tight-lipped and—well—stuffy.

Americans are always polite about Canadians. In thirty years of mingling with them, I've heard only one American make a rude remark about Canadians: he said they were backward. But he was an elephant man at a circus, a violent breed who hated everybody, including other elephant men and elephants, and who shout and swear a lot and threaten to attack and are always in a rage, like cooks. ("How would you like to have to get up at four in the morning and get five elephants into a truck?" one man asked me.) But Americans, if pressed, will give their impression of Canadian speech. When they do, they sound like old-time vaudeville performers imitating a Scotsman, saying, well, it's mainly the way you folk say "oot" and "aboot" and "hoose," a performance often given a chilly reception by the Canadian who asked for it, because Canadians don't sound like that to Canadians, any more than an American sounds strange to an American when he says "howze" for "house."

A while ago I joined a group of Canadians who had come with their families to watch the launching of a Canadian communications satellite at Cape Canaveral, where the U. S. National Aeronautics and Space Administration charges around $7,500,000 to fire things like this into space. Up on the press stand, American newsmen and radio men were cavorting around smoking cigars and wearing funny bowler hats. Below, the Canadians stood silently on a grassy hill like a Viking burial mound, looking east. They wore business suits, or blue blazers and white shoes, like commodores of yacht clubs.

I went up to two men and said I was a Canadian and they turned and looked at me as if thinking: "That may be, but it's a bit boastful to mention it." Then one said he was born in Ottawa, and stopped talking, as if that was all anybody needed to know about anybody. The other said he was from Montreal and stopped talking. We all stood there looking along a swathe cut like a ski run through the scrub, toward a light flashing at the base of the Thor-Delta that stood on pad 17B, two miles away, like a piece of white chalk. Four boat-tailed grackles flew across our line of vision toward a little lake, but nobody mentioned it.

I moseyed off and introduced myself to an executive and told him that I came from Canada and he smiled and said, is that so, but didn't say anything else, leaving me feeling as if I were trying to get a car started in February. A ring-billed gull flew toward the missile, which still stood there steaming lazily between the trellis work of two big reddish gantries that loomed against a grey haze out over the ocean. We could see the Canadian flag floodlit on the side of the missile, and the executive and I stood staring at it, stonily, not speaking, as if it would be a bit emotional to reveal that we had something in common.

The speakers were announcing things like "We are at T minus seven minutes and holding." It was clouding up. A cool wind was coming from the north, from about the direction of Ottawa, and the speaker announced that the hold would last until a big black cloud passed over us. While we waited, I had a vision of the Canadian satellite which before long would be floating through space primly sending back messages over a distance of 22,300 miles in a faintly clipped accent which would sound Scottish to American communications people below. On the Canadian satellite everything would be neat and buttoned up. It would probably be wearing a blazer with a school crest on the breast pocket and maintaining a stiff reserve toward the other satellites—the Russian satellite, breaking open a bottle of vodka and taking off its shoes and pounding a heel on its antenna, and the U.S. satellite smoking a cigar. Then the voice on the speaker was counting again, down to two minutes, one minute . . . four seconds, three seconds, two, one . . .

I've seen two rockets go up from a distance of thirty miles, and one from a distance of ten miles. This was the first I'd seen from two miles. It still looked small and thin in the distance (it was 116 feet high) and it was hard to believe that it would do more than emit a puff of smoke and sound like a Honda. But when someone pushed the button and the Delta let loose 489,000 pounds of thrust and started its way against the pull of gravity, it was as if someone suddenly opened the gates of hell. There was such a savage roar the sky seemed to be coming down on us. Somebody said, "Jesus!" It was me. I had to take my binoculars off the sight. It was like looking right into the sun and watching it fall toward me, an awesome effect caused by the fact that the thing was now overhead, clawing its way upward.

Within seconds a calm settled over the fields and the pond. A plume of black smoke drifted south. The rocket disappeared into a cloud, to reappear as a pinpoint of light. We all walked back to the buses. A Canadian in a Glen Urquhart check jacket opposite me said, "That was very successful." His wife smiled faintly. Then a NASA attendant up by the driver picked up a speaker and congratulated Canada, and all the Canadian youngsters on the bus started to cheer. They whistled. They yelled. They clapped. "I'm still shaking," a plump girl of six or seven kept saying. I was a bit wound up myself from excitement, but trying not to show it, not quite sure how it would go over with the other Canadians.

31

The Drive-in Church
Welcomes Winter Visitors

Travel is loosening roots, breaking up cultures and contributing to a worldwide tendency to accept change and shifting standards and perpetual motion. A lot of people, for instance, feel that the church should move with the times to accommodate travelers, as it has done to accommodate the mass migration of the northern half of the North American continent to the South in the winter time, which now just about empties many northern villages. Churches have been arranged to suit this restless legion of motorists, so that all they need to do to go to church is take their foot off the accelerator for an hour, and I, for one, am not so sure we have gained by it. Sometimes I think the church would have a better chance of survival if it stood still, the way it used to, like a rock.

A while ago I went to a drive-in church located in a strip of motels and steakhouses, with a painting of Jesus kneeling opposite a laundromat. There was a big sign like the ones outside drive-in movies, which announced the sermon and, along with the local chamber of commerce, welcomed the winter visitors. Through no fault of the congregation, any feeling of spirituality was diluted by the environment to the strength of watery orange juice.

I watched one silver-haired gent in a Plymouth with Ohio plates, who, during the Lord's Prayer, sat there with one arm over the seat looking exactly as if he were getting an oil change. While someone behind a kind of broadcast booth window read a psalm over the speakers (which were handed to the motorists at the gate, like hymn books) about a bridegroom striding from his house, everyone near me was distracted by a girl with a bare midriff striding toward the doughnut and coffee bar. A man stood in the sun having a cigarette and looking up at a DC-9 that passed during the singing of "I Am Thine, O Lord."

A case may be made that the outward surroundings have nothing to do with worship, but they do. Among other things, we are creatures of the senses. Automobiles have an unavoidably unholy appearance, and the feeling from looking at 418 of them is the same feeling as the one you get looking at a parking lot. Besides, when you're sitting in your car, you don't kneel, stand, close your eyes, or do anything different physically than you did last Tuesday at a hamburger drive-in. Everyone had been handed a wafer and a tiny paper cup of grape juice for holy communion, but the symbolism is somehow lost as you sit there alone in your car, and drop the empty cup in your trash bag, and sit looking at your mileage, fighting off worries about whether you could get another 10,000 miles without an engine overhaul.

It was all so much a part of the times that it often was indistinguishable in feeling from any other gathering, say, a Kiwanis luncheon. Some time later, electronic church bells rang over the speaker, somebody sang, "The place where I worship is the wide open spaces," and somebody thanked the local chamber of commerce for making the Visitors welcome, and the Visitors thanked the local townspeople for making them welcome. There were eight mentions of hands across borders, and a past president of a supermarket chain blessed the Visitors by tape recorder, and there was an announcement of a future dinner at a Holiday Inn and another about everyone meeting afterward at a nearby steakhouse. Car motors started as the choir sang, "Sing them over again to me, those wonderful words of life." A few cars wouldn't start and the drivers sat with bowed heads listening to their struggling motors and not looking very spiritual.

There was a line-up for coffee and doughnuts. A woman said, without punctuation, "That was a good sermon they're going to run out of coffee before I get there," to the minister. He stood outside the snack bar wearing a smart shirt with a collar with a design like little pink mooses all over it, and fancy sport shoes, shaking hands and greeting people who called him "Mel," and occasionally giving one of the male members of the congregation a bluff little swat on the shoulder like a happy quarterback. I got talking to a Visitor in a blue tie and powder-blue cardigan with an emblem on the pocket, who explained to me that this was a great way to get people out to worship who didn't like getting out of their cars. I stayed till all the cars were gone, and realized that nothing much had happened but a pleasant Sunday morning drive.

I found myself thinking, a bit defensively, of the stiff-backed, starched and blue-serged church of my boyhood, and the grim, grey-haired brewers and brickmakers belting out hymns with a braying, frightening bass. It's true that in its extreme forms religion in those days caused psychological scars that are still giving psychiatrists work today, but it wasn't all like that. And I'll say one thing—when you came out from listening to an hour and a half's impassioned sermon by a minister with his hair in his eyes, you at least knew you'd been exhorted to a better life, and perhaps came out with some new ideas. The sermon I'd listened to was easy and pleasant to take—all about the distances of stars—but it seemed to leave no impression on the people turning in their speakers at the gate as they drove out.

Just one other person was left around the snack bar when I was ready to leave, a very pleasant woman with short hair like yellow seaweed and thick glasses. When I asked her how she enjoyed the sermon she said, fine, and that she came from Chicago and wasn't married and that she'd rather make music than babies and that she'd tried to drink herself to death once—"But all it gave me was brain damage and a nasty disposition," she said cheerfully, and bent over to pick something up, saying that she'd been eating too many doughnuts. I had a brief conversation with a man with thinning hair who sat in his car with the engine running, ready to go. He said he spent a lot of his time travelling and that this time last year he'd been in Portugal, where he had a girl friend who used to bring him his beer balanced on top of her head. There was another car with a sticker on the bumper saying, "If you don't like cops, next time you're in trouble call a hippy."

I heard another man say to a fellow motorist, just as he pulled away, "I don't know why he would have quoted Plato. Did you know Plato was queer? They don't tell you everything at college." Then he drifted off over the field, headed back for outer space for all I know. A gull soared over the empty drive-in lot, looking for something to eat, and I left feeling that the church had moved with the times so fast it had never been there.

32

The See-a-Real-Glacier Tour

If it hasn't happened already, people will soon be blaming things like floods and hurricanes and extra cold winters on the amount of travelling people are doing, and the technology that makes travel possible. A while ago I was talking about the rising levels of the Great Lakes with a tall, gaunt, long-jawed municipal worker in green overalls who stopped shovelling up some leaves, stared silently down at me through pale-blue eyes, looking like the preacher in *Moby Dick,* then jabbed his finger toward the sky and said, "It's those things they're sending up," leaving the thought dangling there like a toppling willow. Then he told me that a man sitting in that truck right over there had a brother-in-law living in Florida who had noticed that every time they sent one of those things up, the Atlantic Ocean rose six inches. I talked to the man in the truck and he said that was right. "It's a known fact," he said. As I left, he called after me, "Then there's the moon."

Then there are all those jumbo jets, and the body temperatures of hundreds of thousands of people floating across the Atlantic, and the heat generated by 50 million cameras taking pictures of the Changing of the Guard, and thinking of this kind of thing I had an urge to take a close look at Lake Ontario, one of the Great Lakes, a chain left by a force that is still essentially a mystery to science. The Great Lakes are five puddles of water so great that their daily runoff would fill a tank the size of a football field sixty-five miles high. They were wiped out several times by re-advancing ice, which lay against their northern boundaries as recently as 10,000 years ago.

To get to Lake Ontario I worked my way through a frightful suburban sprawl of parking lots, apartment buildings and general highway junk, and came out at one of the most spectacular reminders of all this, some high, sheer cliffs. These are among the most famous ice-age deposits in the world, the remains of a delta that was laid down 12,000 years ago in an ancestral Lake Ontario, and is now eroded into spectacular pinnacles of sand and clay.

A bit to the west the slopes are partly wooded, and with caution you can work your way down to where the waves break far below. It takes about fifteen minutes, as you make sure of your handholds, keeping your grip on a fistful of grass or burdock or a branch, or, about thirty feet from the bottom, some bulrushes. You stop now and then to make sure you remember the route back so you won't find yourself trapped down there. A red-winged blackbird floated beneath me, its red epaulets showing, and circled out over the glinting water. A breeze rustled the poplars on the brink above. Clinging there like an old root myself, I felt a bit giddy as I looked into the lake. It wouldn't take much to start you talking to yourself like a mountain climber as you search for the best route. "Ja! The north face might go, if we take the first cwm."

At the bottom I sat on a fat, warm log amid a tangle

of driftwood. I was going to make a fire, but it was too breezy in the only spot where I could build one, and the only sheltered spot was a bit too eerie, with the great greasy clay cliffs towering above as if ready to slide, which they do periodically, eating into real estate at the rate (in some places) of around six feet a year.

I sat there for a while with the spray from the waves hitting my face, getting the feeling that Nature was quietly waiting while man fussed around with his high-rise buildings and expressways. Nobody knows why the glaciers came, or why they left. Right now they may have reached their maximum retreat. Tomorrow they may start to come back, heading toward skyscrapers, which they'd level like wheat.

It was very silent. Thunderclouds were appearing over the cliffs above, and there were dark purple streaks on the lake. I started back up, spurred on by visions of myself being found perfectly preserved in ice, notebook in hand, in the year 10,000, by a group of tourists on a See-a-Real-Glacier tour. From South America or China.

33

Less Speed, More Travel

Whether man will be able to salvage something of the spirit of travel from the travel industry is a problem he'll soon face, just as he now faces the problems of salvaging the city from the apartment industry, and rescuing youth from the youth industry. In a magazine I picked up this morning in a travel agency, there were 106 pages of "Guaranteed Holidays," each giving the statistics on holidays in places like Martinique with all the romance of a car-parts manual: The people. The climate. What to wear. Food and Drink. Night Life. Shopping. Each one gave you the urge not to go there if you could help it. *Holiday* magazine, which used to run fine moody articles on exotic lands, now looks like something given away in a supermarket (although it costs $1.00) and is made up of travel ads and articles on subjects like condominiums, or "The Amazing Mini-Motorhome," priced between $6,000 and $14,000, which one writer said was the fastest growing recreation vehicle in the country. Newspaper travel pages are going in more and more for stimulating titles like "Tying One on in Tasmania" or "Girl Watching Down Under."

Yet man has an innate love of romance and adventure, mystery and magic. One thing we're going to have to do to recapture the romance of travel is to concentrate less on speed and distance and more on sinking back into the present and absorbing the texture of some of the places we are flying over or by-passing on turnpikes. One of the most enjoyable travel experiences I've had for some time was walking through a village (a world we're all forgetting) in which the entire main street was about half a mile long. A line of laundry was blowing beside a potato patch and two women with a little fat terrier sat on a porch staring at me. You could hear individual voices right across the village. There was a sharp, sweet smell of woodsmoke and the only sound was that of the sprocket of a kid's bike which could be heard right across town.

It was a soft summer evening. Inside the only grocery store, the proprietor, a man with white hair and a white apron, was giving all his attention to a little girl who had come in with a nickel, and there took place a scene as exotic as a rain dance. "Can I be of some assistance," he said to the kid, as if she were going to buy a Buick. "We've got these jawbreakers for a penny, and some one-cent bubble gum." He studied the girl for the first flutter of interest. He turned to me. "I like to help them spread their money around a bit," he said. "We've got strawberry-flavored licorice twizzlers and rope twists. These peanuts are five cents." The youngster finally bought a five-cent package of Sun-Maid raisins and left, as silently as a resident of a rain forest. It was a sight to calm the nerves of the 2,600 travel addicts recently described by a Washington, D.C., Travelers Aid worker as people who handle their anxieties and emotional tensions by constant travel and who are hard to treat, the report said, because they don't stay in one place long enough to be treated.

Modern mankind will have to be on guard against the allurements of technology, like that of easily operated color cameras that enable the tourist to take hundreds of slides of places to avoid looking at them, listening to them or thinking about them. I've done my share of photographing monasteries, for instance, then putting the slides in a trunk (which goes into storage because I'm off to some other exotic place) and forgetting that I have them. But I never really saw a monastery until I stayed for a couple of days, as a visitor, at the monastery near Oka, Quebec, run by the Trappists, who date back to the Benedictine monks of sixth-century Europe and became the dominant "white monks" of the twelfth and thirteenth centuries.

I've flown 5,000 miles with less sense of undergoing a new experience than I had getting up at three-thirty on a chilly fall morning and, sitting alone in a dark church balcony, half awake, my stomach empty, my mind full of thoughts I hadn't had for years, looking down on fifty-one white-robed silent monks entering the church one by one in silence, draped in long white cowls. There was a rustle of robes. A steam pipe plinked and there was a bit of nose blowing and a cough or two. The tower bells rang, the sound coming softly into the old stone building, and the monks' voices raised in a chant, without harmony, all singing in unison following a melodic line, inviting mankind to praise God and then singing the invitatory "Be joyful and full of gladness for your name is written in heaven." These men are genuinely dedicated to a cause that brings none of the usual earthly rewards. They've vowed to live a life of poverty, and to remain in the same monastery, work-

ing in the fields, driving tractors, making cheese, raking onions, serving meals, working in the stables, until
they grow old and die. They're not trying to escape
reality, but to find what they believe to be the only
reality—knowledge of God and, through that knowledge, love of man.

Later, I strolled over to a wooded area and sat down
in an old wooden chair beneath some maples and oaks
on a hillock overlooking a pasture and apple orchard.
A road to the new international airport at Ste. Scholas-
tique would soon cut right through the property, sepa-
rating the monastery from a field that that summer was
planted in rye. I sat there thinking of my own flight
back to Toronto, with all those businessmen with black
attaché cases, who would be reading articles on how
to get the most out of your sales force, and not looking
out the windows at the pink granite islands of the St.
Lawrence or speaking to one another. I wondered just
what they, and I, were trying to accomplish.

I thought of the hundreds of thousands of tourists
at that moment moving around the world, and of the
moment in a plane when corks are popping and the
passengers are beginning to move up and down the
aisles. I thought of early Sunday morning in Las Vegas
with the slot machines gleaming like altars, and plump
cold-eyed broads in tarty stockings calling the customers "dear"; and of Roman cab drivers pounding the
tops of their cabs and shouting, "It's a taxi, a taxi, a
taxi; it has an engine and four wheels," and looking
furious; and of Dutch baggage-room men muttering,
"God-damned Canadians!"

I thought of the fellow tourists who have come briefly
into my life and told me those little stories that people,
out of context and knowing they're going to vanish

soon, tell one another—I thought of one man who, for some reason, I remember as clearly as the sun setting over Sounion, telling me in a compulsive monologue about how he loved to travel every year and how his wife left him with nothing but a note saying, "Get someone else to darn your sox. Don't try to find me." and how—boy!—leading a single life was great, and you always have something to look forward to, like going to Japan next year. He disappeared down the station platform with the breeze from a passing train ruffling his thinning hair, and didn't recognize me five minutes later, when I found myself beside him at a station information counter where he was explaining to the girl that he didn't want to be taken, but he didn't want to sleep in a dump, either, because he was there essentially for a good time, he said, and it would be foolish not to have a good time for the sake of a dollar or two. The girl kept saying patiently, "If you'll just tell me what you want I'll try to get it for you." I got the feeling he didn't know, any more than most of us, when we set out to see the world.